In his latest book, *People,* Dickerman draws from his ministry and skillfully lays a solid foundation addressing the important issues of spiritual warfare like a wise master builder. All the while he places top priority on the atoning work of Christ on the cross by providing the biblical and commonsense tools of how to fight our enemy and his demonic powers by the authority and Lordship of Christ. The author rightfully points out, "There is no power that is not subject to His (Christ) control and beneath His name." Dickerman's book provides the spiritual keys necessary for every believer desiring to live an overcoming life. It is a must-read for every Christian seeking God's victory over the forces of darkness for their lives.

—Marcus D. Lamb
President, founder, and CEO, Daystar Television Network

Don Dickerman has a clear understanding of the spirit realm. He is a specialist in deliverance. He has the Word of God and personal experience concerning the supernatural. Don is not one who just talks about deliverance but one who does it with great success and is seeing changed forever. In this book he shares many key truths and much needed wisdom that is vital in deliverance ministry. This book is an essential read for leaders and laypeople who are in the ministry of setting people free.

—Rev. Earl Inman
Freedom Victory Centre
Oshawa, Ontario, Canada

Don Dickerman has done a wonderful exposition of the spirit realm in this book. This is a practical book, written to empower its readers to successfully navigate the spirit realm without casualties. I am intrigued at the details Don went into, with powerful illustrations, giving to the dos and don'ts of winning in spiritual warfare without compromising the theological integrity of the subject. It is obvious that the greatest weapon of the adversary is the ignorance of people, which is exactly what Don has set himself to dislodge. With this book both clergy and laity can successfully navigate the cumbersome terrain of the spirit with proficiency. I strongly recommend it for your spiritual enrichment and advancement.

—Dave Arogbonlo
Senior pastor, RCCG—Living Word Chapel
Houston, Texas

For more than twenty years I have had the opportunity to get to know personally some of the greatest ministers of deliverance. I have continually looked for ways and ministries that I could put on the air on our daily radio broadcasts. One of the quickest ways to get our program canceled was to incorporate the "ministry of deliverance." I used such phrases as "inner healing" to stay afloat.

Deliverance is not a bad word or a mysterious practice. In the New Testament the Greek word used for deliverance is the same word used for salvation.

I needed a strong, stable, gentle spokesman who could teach inner healing as deliverance and still stay "on the air." Along came a man who had experienced more than twenty-five thousand deliverances in his ministry. Don Dickerman was and is that man.

Don made it clear to our audience that ignorance, lies, and fear among believers allow the enemy, demons, to continue to manipulate and oppress them even after they have experienced the new birth. I have found that Don's teaching and books can clearly put the ministry of deliverance into your hands. Don Dickerman's books take the mystery and fear out of the ministry of deliverance and deliver a one-two punch to our enemy.

—Dr. Jim Rome
Global Air Force Radio
www.GlobalAirForce.net

Every once in a while there is a resource that speaks so directly to issues facing the church in this day and age that it becomes an absolute must-have for all Christians and church leaders. This book will open your eyes to the realm of the supernatural and give spiritual insight into the application of angelic hosts and principalities and powers unlike anything you've ever read. This book brings incredible confirmation to the verse of Scripture in Hebrews 13:2 that declares, "Do not forget to entertain strangers, for by so doing some have unwittingly entertained angels" (NKJV).

The personal testimonies and transparency of Don Dickerman's understanding of the spiritual atmosphere around us should cause everyone to draw closer to God's anointing and presence in these last days. This book brought connection and blessing to things in my personal life and ministry we all have experienced and may never have been able to explain or understand! *It's a powerful book!*

—Rev. James Boyd
Pastor, Faith Tabernacle Assembly of God
Klamath Falls, Oregon

The godly wisdom revealed by Brother Dickerman in this writing is priceless. Both the layperson and the scholar must not pass up the opportunity to obtain the clear balance of experience, wisdom, and knowledge this book brings to the church in an area where many have groped and gasped for an effective, proficient, comprehensive, and biblical approach to deliverance.

—Bishop Annas Aytch, PhD
Pastor, Covenant Ministries Church International
Huntsville, AL
Author, *Living Supernaturally—Gaining Your Inheritance*

PEOPLE

PIGS

&

PRINCIPALITIES

DON DICKERMAN

CHARISMA
HOUSE

PEOPLE, PIGS, AND PRINCIPALITIES by Don Dickerman
Published by Charisma House
Charisma Media/Charisma House Book Group
600 Rinehart Road
Lake Mary, Florida 32746
www.charismahouse.com

Cover design by
Design Director: Bill Johnson

Visit the author's website at http://www.dondickerman.net/.

Library of Congress Cataloging-in-Publication Data:
An application to register this book for cataloging has been
submitted to the Library of Congress.
International Standard Book Number: 978-1-62136-530-3
E-book ISBN: 978-1-62136-531-0

While the author has made every effort to provide accurate
telephone numbers and Internet addresses at the time of
publication, neither the publisher nor the author assumes any
responsibility for errors or for changes that occur after publication.

First edition

14 15 16 17 18 —9 8 7 6 5 4 3 2 1
Printed in the United States of America

Contents

Foreword

As a mental health professional of thirty years I have witnessed firsthand the foundation of truth you will find in the pages of *People, Pigs, and Principalities*. In this eye-opening book Don Dickerman outlines the source, nature, and consequences of demonic influences, shedding light on the kind of darkness I see inhabiting the hearts, minds, and souls of men, women, and adolescents who turn to me desperate for help, hope, and healing.

When I founded The Center for Counseling and Health Resources in 1984, it was on the basis of a unique approach to treatment—whole-person health, addressing the physical, mental, emotional, relational, and, last but not least, *spiritual* aspects of a person's life.

I have seen people come through our doors spiritually bankrupt. A number of them have been in and out of treatment programs for years, none of which made a lasting impact in what I believe to be a direct result of neglecting the spiritual side.

As Don Dickerman touches upon throughout this book, the deliverance ministry he has been engaged in for going on twenty years is anchored in shedding light on the truth, for, as he writes, "It is truth that enables us to be free."

Believing lies empowers dark forces, a truth all its own,

which I see manifested in the lives of those I treat for mental health conditions.

The longer you hold on to a lie, the harder it is to let go. And, sadly, many people have been holding on to lies all their lives—lies that feed the self-doubt and self-loathing associated with the addiction, depression, anxiety, and eating disorders that plague millions around the world. Their perception of the world, of others, and of themselves is distorted. They see, hear, feel, and believe not what's true but what they're *afraid* is true. And the difference between them is often one between peace and torment.

In *People, Pigs, and Principalities* Don Dickerman explains how demons are masters of *perception deception*. Demonic influences not only need us to believe a lie, but they also know how to twist and turn our hearts, minds, and souls into fertile ground for these lies to take root and to grow.

Though the whole-person approach to treatment is the key, there have been times with severe addictions and depression that we have witnessed deliverance from demonic influences as the completion step to a person's healing.

All of that said, the author is quick to note in chapter 2 of this book that there is one place demonic influences hold no sway:

> While the unclean spirits may possess an area of a person's life, genuine possession by demons cannot happen to a Christian, for possession is ownership, and we are owned by the Lord Jesus.... The spirits dwell in the flesh and/or the soul, but never in the spirit, for that is where the Holy Spirit lives.

I am further comforted by the attention Don Dickerman pays to angels through inspiring accounts involving those closest to him. After all, no book about demonic influences that work for evil should be complete without the inclusion of *angelic* influences that work for God.

—GREGORY L. JANTZ, PHD
FOUNDER, THE CENTER FOR COUNSELING AND HEALTH RESOURCE

Dr. Gregory Jantz is an internationally recognized best-selling author of twenty-six books and a mental health expert. He is also the founder of The Center for Counseling and Health Resources, Inc. Known as "A Place of Hope," it is a leading health care facility based in Seattle. The treatment center offers therapy programs for individuals, teens, families, and even celebrities who struggle with addiction, stress, abuse, depression, PTSD, weight loss, unhealthy body image, relationship problems, and more.

Introduction

WHY AM I INTERESTED?

RECENTLY A MINISTER and his wife from Canada were in our office for deliverance. After the sessions we had some conversation, and I was asked, maybe for the hundredth time, "How did you get started in deliverance ministry?"

Boy, that's a long and involved story including many, many miles, hundreds of prisons, and thousands of lives—but I want to share a *significant* part of that answer with you.

I was preaching at the Federal Correctional Institution in Three Rivers, Texas. The facility prison is located about halfway between San Antonio and Corpus Christi just off Interstate 37. This is a medium-security complex of about fourteen hundred inmates. The chaplain, who was my friend, was a gracious host. There was something very unusual in the chapel service that evening. A uniformed correctional officer was seated among the inmates and was worshipping with them. That just never happens. If there is an officer present, it is because he has been assigned to the chapel.

It is very unusual for an officer to mingle with the inmates. I found out later that he was off duty and studying to become a federal prison chaplain or counselor. After the service he told the officer on duty that he would escort me to my car because he wanted to talk with me.

When the service was over, this officer came up to me and shook my hand. I recall that the evening was brisk and the sky was very clear and crisp. It was one of those *perfect evenings*. The officer told me of his call to the ministry and of his desire to become a federal prison chaplain. We visited some more after reaching the prison parking lot, and after we prayed together, I headed back to Corpus Christi to the south, and he headed toward his home in Beeville to the east. I stopped at a convenience store for a soft drink and a snack before getting on Interstate 37 to drive back to Corpus Christi, where I was staying.

As I pulled up at the convenience store/service station, I was unaware that the officer pulled in right behind me. Before I could get out of my car, he came running over and told me, with great excitement, that God had given him a vision about me, and he *had* to share it with me. He said, "I would have followed you all the way to Corpus to tell you about the vision." He was so excited I could feel and sense that God had spoken to him. This is what he told me:

> I saw you standing in this big black pot, and there was oil bubbling all around you, not boiling, just bubbling. All around the pot there was a sea of people, as far as you could see, and they were all sick. The stench of their sickness was nauseating as it went up to the heavens. Then the oil began to bubble up and cover you, and as it ran from your head and down your arms and touched the people, they were healed! Get ready, brother, God's *fix'in* to pour it out on you!

I cannot adequately describe what I felt. It was like I was just bathed in God's glory. While he was sharing the words with me, I sensed the presence of God's Spirit stirring in me. I knew these words were from God. But I didn't know what to do with the words from the vision. As I drove back to Corpus Christi, tears continually moistened my eyes. There was subdued excitement in my spirit. I had seen thousands receive Christ as Savior, perhaps one hundred thousand or more, but I had never seen anyone healed or delivered of demons. Actually, what I had been taught did not *fit* with the word given to me. I had been taught that the gifts of the Spirit had died out with the apostles. I had been taught that the gifts would cease "when that which is perfect has come" (1 Cor. 13:10), and that this "perfect" meant God's Word. Since we have God's Word, then there is no need for the gifts of the Spirit to operate—that's what I had been taught.

I wish I had been more open to scriptural truth and not so heavily influenced by denominational tradition; I missed some of the greatest truths! I didn't know how to make this vision happen. I didn't know how to give altar calls except for salvation. Soon I would find out I didn't need to know.

Not long after this incredible experience I was back in that same area of the state preaching at a state prison in Beeville. That unit of the Texas Department of Criminal Justice is named the Garza West facility. About five hundred inmates were in the gym that night, and perhaps as many as two-thirds of the men had answered the altar call. When the service was over, the men returned to their seats and were called back to their housing area by dorm location. As they filed out in single file, one of the men stepped from the line and approached the chaplain.

I had noticed this young man during the service; he sat on the front row and stared at me as though he *saw something*. There was sort of a look of wonderment on his face as I ministered. The chaplain brought him over to me and said, "This inmate has a word for you from the Lord, something the Lord showed him as you preached."

He still had this look on his face. He said, "Sir, God told me something to tell you." He continued: "While you were preaching, I saw something, and God told me something to tell you." He moved beside me and asked me to stretch my arm forward, straight out toward the now empty seats. He placed his arm on top of mine and said, "God told me to tell you that as you extend your hand, so will He extend His." He seemed puzzled, like he was just passing on a message. "Do you know what that means, sir?"

"Yes," I told him, "yes, I do. Thanks for sharing that with me." When I left the prison that night, again the Holy Spirit of God just seemed to cover me. It is so holy that it is very difficult to share. Tears again filled my eyes simply from the glory of His presence. I knew God had spoken to me again, and I am just unable to describe how humbling this was and is to me.[1]

Before there were demons, there were angels. Before there were angels, there was God. We actually don't know much about what happened prior to our present creation. It seems the more we study and learn about God and His marvelous works, the more we realize that we really don't know much at all. I never thought I would be dealing with this subject of principalities and powers, angels and demons. I don't think I ever heard a preacher or Sunday school teacher even address the subject.

As I reflect now on my memories of being saved and growing up in the church, of my experiences in Bible schools and seminaries, I do not recall any pastor or teacher approaching the subject other than general mentions of Satan. I guess you could accurately say that I was ignorant of the subject regarding angels and demons.

I knew the spirit realm existed, but knew little about it and had only a passing interest in this area of the supernatural. I'm pretty sure that many of you could say the same thing. In Christian circles there are several categories of views on God's work today. Concerning miracles, there are at least three:

1. Those who don't believe God ever did miracles

2. Those who believe He did miracles then but doesn't do them now

3. Those who believe He did and He does!

I fall into the last category. When it comes to the spirit realm, there are probably many more divisions. There are those who don't believe in any kind of spirit world, and some who believe in angels, and some who believe in angels and demons. Some believe that angels and demons were once active in the affairs of men but not now, and others believe that angels are still active but demons are not. Some believe that if you are a Christian, you cannot be demonized. Some believe that someone can be harassed by demons, but no demon can enter into our lives. That includes just a few of the so-called born-again believers.

I believe there are angelic and demonic powers actively involved in the affairs of mankind. I will be sharing some of the many experiences I have had. It is the purpose of demon powers to *war against* the children of God and to oppose the work of God. Angels, as part of their creative purpose, *minister for* God's people. This phrase might even be a summary of this book—angels minister for believers; demons war against believers. Angels serve God; demons oppose God.

Demons war against. Angels minister for. War against. Minister for. This is an unmistakable truth from God's Word.

I would rather have an unclean pig in my house than an unclean spirit in my tabernacle. "What's the deal with *pigs*?" people ask. *Pigs* represent unclean spirits. I could probably use a host of different words to do that. My deceased friend Frank Hammond also used the word *pigs* to describe the demonic spirits in his book *Pigs in the Parlor*.[2] Seems everyone knows without an explanation, but still many people ask me.

I actually wrote and recorded a song about this, and you can go to our website (www.dondickerman.com) and request a copy if you like. The words, which oversimplify the message, are:

> What would you do if a pig moved in?
> Through an open door, they're on your floor.
> When pigs move in
> Stinking up your life, going through your stuff,
> Well, when ya gonna say to them,
> Enough is enough?
>
> Messing up your house,
> Boy, they're wearing you down.
> You got to tell that pig
> He can't stay around.
>
> Through an open door, tell me what would you do
> If an unclean pig moved right in with you?
> He's got a messy snout, big, ugly, and stout,
> I'm not sure, but I bet you'd wanna keep him out.
>
> Closing the door, now, that's the big thing,
> Confessing and receiving in Jesus' name.
> What do you do when the pigs move in?
> In the name of Jesus,
> You send them back to their pen.

Chapter 1

WHAT ARE PRINCIPALITIES AND POWERS?

THE PHRASE "PRINCIPALITIES and powers" occurs six times in the Bible, always in the King James Version and its derivatives. There are some versions that translate it variously as "rulers and authorities," "forces and authorities," and "rulers and powers." The principalities and powers of Satan are in a similar structure of power and authority as the holy angels who did not rebel and oppose God. These demonic creatures wield power in the unseen realms to oppose anything and anyone that is of God.

The first mention of principalities and powers is in Romans 8:37–39:

> Nay, in all these things we are more than conquerors through him that loved us. For I am persuaded, that neither death, nor life, nor angels, nor principalities, nor powers, nor things present, nor things to come, nor height, nor depth, nor any other creature, shall be able to separate us from the love of God, which is in Christ Jesus our Lord.

These verses are about the victory we have in Christ. We are "more than conquerors" because no force—not life, not death, not angels, not demons, indeed nothing—can separate us from the love of God, which is in Christ Jesus. It seems that the "powers" referred to here are those with miraculous powers, whether false teachers and prophets or the very demonic entities that empower them. It is clear that no power, whatever it may be, can separate us from the love of God. "In Christ Jesus" is an important wording here, for it is in Christ that our victory is assured. It is in His name that we can obtain and maintain victory.

The second mention of principalities and powers is found in Ephesians 1:20–21:

> Which he wrought in Christ, when he raised him from the dead, and set him at his own right hand in the heavenly places, far above all principality, and power, and might, and dominion, and every name that is named, not only in this world, but also in that which is to come.

I like that it says that Christ is "far above" all principality—not just above, but far above! Not just principalities and powers and might and dominion, but "ALL" principalities and power and might and dominion—*all* of them. This is an overwhelming signal that every power is beneath the *name* of Jesus!

Ephesians 3:10–11 presents the third picture of principalities and powers in the heavenly realms:

> To the intent that now unto the principalities and powers in heavenly places might be known by the church the manifold wisdom of God, according to the eternal purpose which he purposed in Christ Jesus our Lord.

Here, it seems the revelation is to the angelic hosts showing the wisdom and purpose of God. Angels, both holy and unholy, observe the glory of God and the preeminence of Christ above all creatures in the church. Verse 10 in the NIV reads, "Now, through the church...," and seems to indicate that God is showing that His redemptive plan includes both Jews and Gentiles. Perhaps the angels, who desire to look into man's salvation, may not have had full knowledge of God's plan, and it is being revealed through the church. These angelic beings, referred to as *principalities and powers*, are divided into two factions—those who remained true to God and those who joined in Satan's rebellion against God.

The fourth reference is in Ephesians 6:12, which declares the battle in which we are engaged:

> For we wrestle not against flesh and blood, but against principalities, against powers, against the rulers of the darkness of this world, against spiritual wickedness in high places.

The NIV records it this way: "For our struggle is not against flesh and blood, but against the rulers, against the authorities, against the powers of this dark world and against the spiritual forces of evil in the heavenly realms." The Amplified reads, "For we are not wrestling with flesh and blood [contending only with physical opponents], but against the despotisms, against the powers, against [the master spirits who are] the world rulers of this present darkness, against the spirit forces of wickedness in the heavenly (supernatural) sphere."

Despotism is an interesting word used to describe these powers and is defined as, "absolute rule in a wicked or oppressive manner." There is a sophisticated hierarchy of evil in the heavenly realm; it is the result of the direction of these spirits that minions of demons are directed toward us. They are always looking for open doors through which to attack.

It is as though we are facing an army of dark powers that have been disarmed from real power. Wouldn't they just kill us all if they could? They attack us through lies, threats and deceptions, sickness and various diseases—always as a result of disobedience in our lives or many times in the lives of our ancestors.

One of the clearest examples would be the generational results that can be visibly observed as a result of incest and inbreeding. What took place before and during one's birth can be manifested in abnormalities that are readily recognized. Sin in the world! Our actions and reactions to the lies and temptations of demons most often determine the outcome. Propaganda in the evil realm is satanic misinformation and is distributed by and through the principalities and powers.

Colossians 1:16 reads:

> For by him were all things created, that are in heaven, and that are in earth, visible and invisible, whether they be thrones, or dominions, or principalities, or powers: all things were created by him, and for him.

This is the fifth mention of principalities and powers. Here is the clear statement that God is the Creator and ruler over all authorities! Whatever power the evil spirits possess, they are always subject to the rule of our sovereign God, who, according to Daniel 4:35 and Isaiah 46:10–11, uses even the wicked for bringing about His perfect plan and purpose.

In Colossians 2:15 we see again that Jesus is the ultimate power over all other powers: "Having disarmed principalities and powers, He made a public spectacle of them, triumphing over them in it" (NKJV). As ancient armies would return to announce their victory, sometimes they returned with the enemies' body armor tied to the horses and the body of the enemy leader strapped to the chariot wheels, making a triumphal entry back into the city. This was a display of public humiliation of the enemy. So Jesus Christ has made a public spectacle of demon powers through His death, burial, and resurrection!

There is no power that is not subject to His control and beneath His name. Principalities and powers, rulers of darkness, and spiritual wickedness in high places have all been disarmed by the cross. The Savior, by His death and resurrection, took dominion from them. I have never encountered a demonic power that does not recognize this as truth. It is in His name that we have victory.

There is reference to principalities and powers in Titus 3:1. Here they refer to those governmental authorities under whom we dwell. They are duly constituted authorities.

By using the phrase "principalities and powers," God's Word is telling us that there is a hierarchical structure to the kingdom of darkness—a sophisticated government where fallen angels, evil spirits, and demons are ranked one above the other according to their power and authority. These evil spirits exercise influence over people, geographical areas, cities, and nations. This evil, Satan-ruled hierarchy is a *copycat* form of government similar to God's.

Contending With the Devil

I think Christians make a mistake when they believe they have been given authority to challenge these powers in the heavenly realm. I will simply ask, "If we have that authority, why then does it not work? And why limit it to a particular location?" If through a human being's declaration to principalities and powers we can change their actions, why not extend it to the whole earth? I have never seen a positive result from Christians engaging in spiritual warfare with heavenly realm powers.

I have seen the opposite happen with churches dissolving, ministries crumbling, and individuals suffering sickness and multitudes of difficulties. Our God-given authority has to do with *individuals*—it is to pray for nations, not against principalities and powers. Jesus sent His disciples to the people, not against heavenly realm powers. He did not bind the evil prince of Jerusalem; instead He admonished us to pray for the peace of Jerusalem. He did not pray against heavenly realm powers; He prayed for people. He sent believers commissioned to preach the good news to nations, not to pray against the demonic powers.

Principalities are the chief rulers of the kingdom of darkness; they are first in rank or power and constitute a high order of evil spirits. Every place you see the word *principality* in the King James Version New Testament, it is the Greek noun *arche,* defined as, "that which is first in time, order, or place." This word is used at least seven times in the Scriptures to denote angelic or demonic rulers. The word *powers* is from the Greek noun *exousia* and means, "one who possesses authority or influence." It is the word used in Ephesians 6:12 to represent the angelic or demonic authorities that operate in the spirit realm.

I was recently in Canada for some deliverance seminars and "Nights of Ministry." One of the ladies I met in Kingston, where there are many prisons, said, "Sometimes my husband and I drive by the Kingston pen and just bind up all of the spirits there." What? I wonder what she was thinking! Did she really believe her "binding up" all of the demons there changed anything? You know it is a troubling doctrine that is being preached and taught today that we have some kind of authority in the heavenlies. Please, if this is so, we should get to the hospitals and psychiatric centers—but it doesn't work, and it is very dangerous and foolish to attempt it. Pick a fight with a principality? Please.

While I was in this same city in Canada, a man who is involved in deliverance ministry told me of a group there that did "prayer marching and pulling down strongholds" in the city. He said they have tried to get him involved, but he feels that what they are doing is not scriptural. He told me there were twenty-five or thirty people who did this. I asked him what kind of success they had experienced after a couple of years. "I don't know of any," he said. "They're all sick or their families are falling apart. I think they have disbanded."

Ephesians 6:12 also speaks about the "rulers of the darkness of this age" (NKJV). To my knowledge, this term is only found in this verse. "Rulers" is translated from the Greek noun *kosmokrator*, which is defined as, "lord of the world, the prince of this age." The god of this world, Satan, is indicated here.

The last group mentioned in Ephesians 6:12 is "spiritual hosts of wickedness" (NKJV), or wicked spirits that operate in high places. Here, the Greek word *epouranios* refers to the dwelling place of God as well as the abode of angels and evil spirits. This also translates to "heavenly places," a sphere of activity or existence that is above that of the earth.

There is an interesting statement in *Vine's Expository Dictionary of New Testament Words*:

> The context ("not against flesh and blood") shows that no earthly potentates are indicated, but spirit powers, who, under the permissive will of God, and in consequence of human sin, exercise satanic and therefore

antagonistic authority over the world in its present condition of spiritual darkness and alienation from God.[1]

How true, "in consequence of human sin"—as given permission by our unconfessed sin! Our ignorant disobedience comes into play here as well. The god of this world is Satan according to the Bible. He has in place a governmental hierarchy doubtlessly patterned after God's with numerous levels of authority and power. I don't know how many levels of demonic bureaucracy would be between Satan and the demons we deal with on our plain, but it is vast.

Think about it for a moment. If you were *god of this earth* what would your governmental organizational chart look like? Would you have a leader established over all the continents? Would you also have them over the seas, the islands, the mountains, and the deserts—OK, in all of the earth? Let's just look at the United States. How many levels between you and the president…a lot? How about your state? How about your county, your city? How about your neighborhood, your block? Do you see how vast the demonic hierarchy would be? Is there at least one demon for every person…more? I will discuss this in a later chapter.

I have been involved in deliverance ministry for a long time. One thing is clear. There are two different models of practice among those who are involved in this kind of ministry. One model is to attack the principalities and powers, and by doing so take back the territory that they have earned. The other model is to deal with individuals who are saved and want to be free from demon powers in their lives. One model works; the other doesn't. One model Jesus endorsed; the other He did not.

Whenever I meet with someone for deliverance, it is always at the individual's request. I'm not a demon slayer looking for people who may need my help. When the person comes to me to be rid of what may have entered his or her life or become attached to it, most often territorial spirits come with them. They come to defend the kingdom they have established. Most always they will be there to make it difficult and to cause doubt, confusion, or fear. They come because they are over the demons to be dealt with in the person. They attempt to block or hinder the deliverance. Often I can sense their presence; there is usually an *attack* on my mind or on the person's mind. I can tell when leading a person in prayer if the demon doesn't want a particular part of the prayer prayed.

Early in my ministry I did not understand this and could not successfully deal with it. One day the Holy Spirit showed me something. This is so important. He showed me how to distinguish between spirits on the inside and demon powers who are present on the outside, generally territorial spirits. Now I first address the outside territorial spirits and determine if they have any legal rights to be there. They will communicate with me through the individual. They are being confronted in the name of Jesus. I command from them their names, the names that are recognized by Jehovah God. Once I get their names, I command that they reveal their creative purpose. For instance I may ask, "When God created you as a holy angel, what did He create you to do?"

An example of the answer that comes would be, "To bring peace." So immediately I know that as a demon he now does the opposite. Remember they oppose God! I also command the demon to reveal his assigned geographical territory on the earth—I know he has one, and I will insist that he reveal it. Generally it will be the same area where the person was born, or perhaps where he or she presently lives.

Recently an eighteen-year-old girl came for deliverance.

In the process I did as I just mentioned. I commanded the name of the territorial spirits present; there were two. They both revealed their names, but she was silent when I commanded that they reveal their geographical territory. She said, "I don't hear anything, but I see trees, lots of trees." When commanding the geographical territory for the other she said, "Now I see cliffs." She was from Oregon, born and raised there. When I commanded the spirits to reveal if their territory was Oregon, they said, "It includes Oregon."

I know this may sound strange to you. I have done this for almost twenty years, and it is always consistent. Now I command the spirits to answer, before Jehovah God, this one question: "Do you have legal permission to be here?" When the answer is no, and it usually is, I command them to return to their place in the heavenlies, to not come back, and to not send others to replace them. They leave. I have documented these events over the years, as I always take notes. I have thousands of names of territorial spirits and their territories. These demons are principalities and powers. I used to try to cast those demons into the abyss. "Not possible," they would respond. "You can send me back to the heavenlies, but you cannot send me to the abyss." Hmm…I learned this to be true. I could, however, clean out the kingdom of demons on the inside or attached and send them to the abyss, and I do.

My point here is that there are two levels of this battle, and until we recognize this, we will not be successful. I also want you to know that I do not carry on conversations with demons, but I do confront them and demand truth from them. In one session similar to the session with the lady from Oregon, one of the territorial spirits boasted of his high rank. I commanded him to reveal where he would be in level of authority beneath Satan. He responded with, "I am three tiers beneath him."

I said, "Will you call him here? I want to ask him something." Immediately the response was, "He won't come."

I said, "You don't even know where he is, do you?"

"No, I don't, but he won't come here."

Interesting, with seven billion people in the world, why would he come here? He has a lofty position in the heavenly realm; he is not omnipresent. He is not in all places, nor can he be in more than one place at a time. His underlings carry out his plans and desires. I could tell you a lot of personal stories to confirm this.

The Man We Call *Legion*

Here is one example from Scripture. On one side of the Sea of Galilee a mother was crying. I believe the father was too. Their son was tormented, and they did not know what to do. There was no psychiatrist or psychologist to consult. Not only was their son tormented, but also he tormented others. He could not live at home; he could not function in society. In today's world he would doubtlessly be in prison or in a secure mental institution. I don't know how old he was or how long he had been in this condition. I do know he had a mother and father. I'm pretty sure they had done all they knew to do. Still, they prayed.

He wandered among the tombs, restless and driven by his tormentors. Each time I read this, I recall a sight I beheld when I was beginning seminary. I worked for the local electric company as a meter reader. Eventually you wind up in everyone's back yard; you see a lot of strange things and meet some strange people. I could take you to this house today in south Fort Worth. It was a corner lot with no fence and had a detached garage that was near the alley and could be entered from the side street.

As I was leaving the yard, I noticed a chain that led into the open garage. As a meter reader you learn to respect what might be on the other end of a chain. As I eased by the garage, I looked to see what was on the other end of the chain. I expected a large dog. But it wasn't. My heart beats heavy even as I write this. It was a man! He was crouched on the ground like an animal. I did not investigate any further. Actually it startled me. I quickly moved to the next house but could not get it off my mind and heart.

I asked fellow workers about it later. Several had seen him in the months before and had reported it. I recall one of the workers said, "Oh, you mean the crazy guy on Davis Avenue." It seemed that the man's parents didn't have the means to hospitalize him or maybe even were ignorant of how to care for him. When they were gone, he was chained in the garage with food and water, and some shade and some shelter. Horrible!

The man with demons in Gadara (Mark 5) must have been similar. I know his parents prayed; I feel certain they did all they could. Maybe the man himself, in a moment of sanity, cried out to God. I believe a prayer was heard when Jesus spoke to His disciples, "Let us cross over to the other side" (Mark 4:35, NKJV). What was on the other side? This man in a hopeless condition!

Not only were there prayers being prayed, but I believe there was also communication going on in the demonic spirit realm. I believe the demons on the inside of this man knew Jesus was coming, because they had been told—warned. They all knew Him. I believe they cried to their principalities and powers, to their territorial spirits asking for help. There is lots of communication going on in the demonic kingdom of darkness.

Perhaps the principalities stirred the storm. They stir storms. Jesus stills them. Notice He did not speak to the principalities but to the storm they had created. He did not bind the prince of the Sea of Galilee, He destroyed their works. That is what the Bible says Jesus came to do. First John 3:8 says, "For this purpose the Son of God was manifested, that He might destroy the works of the devil" (NKJV).

There are many lessons to be learned in this account. Jesus spoke to the demons in the man. He demanded the name of the demons. In private He commanded demons to speak; in public He forbade them to speak. I find the same thing true in our ministry. We don't have conversation; we have confrontation! They knew who He was; they still do. They obeyed His command, and they still bow in His name.

We don't know much about the rest of the story, except the man was completely rid of demons. Where he had been naked, out of his mind, and a problem to others, he was now clothed, in his right mind, and wanting to follow Jesus.

> Casting down arguments and every high thing that exalts itself against the knowledge of God, bringing every thought into captivity to the obedience of Christ.
> —2 CORINTHIANS 10:5, NKJV

Look what Jesus did for the Gadarene; He restored him to his right mind. Without doubt the most difficult of individuals whom we deal with are those who have been diagnosed with mental disorders. If it was like some of the spiritual warfare movements teach, then we could just circle the mental institutions and bind the entire kingdom of mind-tormenting spirits.

This is a tough one for several reasons. I am somewhat acquainted with it. My mother was diagnosed as *paranoid schizophrenic*. She attempted suicide nine times in a six-week period. She was tormented in her mind. This was before I knew about deliverance as I do now. Since her death I have many times tried to discover what may have happened in her life that could have allowed this. I don't know. Her two sisters committed suicide. If they were abused as children, I don't know about it; none of my relatives know about it. While I suspect that may have been the problem, I don't know.

I can't find anything in her ancestry that helps me to answer the mystery—but there was a source. It was the work of demons. My friend the late Frank Hammond was convinced in his ministry that *rejection* is at the root of paranoia and schizophrenia. I have had many experiences to confirm that, however, there may be multiple things that come together to bring this about. Delusion is maximum deception. *Paranoia* is defined as, "a mental condition characterized by delusions of persecution, unwarranted jealousy, or exaggerated self-importance. It is unjustified suspicion and mistrust of others." "Exaggerated self-importance"…I see this a lot in the ministry. Unfortunately it also is often among those who claim to be "God-called" ministers.

The paranoia is so strong that to the individual it is real. He or she sees something or hears something. Something is going on. Again, people say it's just in their minds—think about that; what is just in their minds?

The question is really not that it is caused by demon powers; rather it is how the demons cause it. Without doubt many people in this condition need medical help. Often the individual needs both spiritual and physiological help. Sometimes the person needs some medical attention so that he or she can be delivered. It is virtually always different.

When a lie has been believed, it is very difficult to deal with demons until the lie has been renounced. The problem here is that the deception is so powerful that the individual does not perceive it to be a lie. He becomes so fully blinded by the lie that he is unable to see the truth. Perhaps he became so comfortable in the lie that he is unwilling to believe the truth. He is convinced that the government is persecuting him or that secret agents are assigned to spy and gather information against him. He is so convinced that it is very difficult for him to confess it as a lie. He often becomes suspicious of you because you don't believe the story.

It is always the same and never the same. It may be the neighbors plotting against him, sometimes coworkers telling false stories about him, or hearing people outside of his house—or in the house. These individuals often are convinced that witches and warlocks are putting curses on them. The torment they feel is real. There is no doubt that what they perceive is very real to them. So the dilemma is how to bring freedom to those suffering from disorders of the mind.

I assure you it is more than simply commanding demons to go in the name of Jesus. If it was that simple, I would be at the mental hospitals right now. I have been there; I have prayed for institutionalized people. I have spent many hours in the psychiatric wings of the prisons; I have heard the demons react when I would walk down the halls or come by their cells. I have heard the screams down the corridors as the sounds from the chapel services spilled into the prison. It is more than just speaking the name of Jesus over a mentally ill person. It is complex, and until the legal rights of those demon powers have been removed (by the individual or parents), freedom does not come.

The name of Jesus will stir them regardless. Demons hate and fear that name. Some people with mental disorders cannot even read the Bible for the torment that comes. Some read it and are only able to see condemnation and judgment. The thing I know is that there is always a root, sometimes many roots. The problem is finding it and removing permissions that demons have gained. The problem is that often the demons have already done their damage, and even when they leave, God's supernatural healing is needed.

One of the things we have experienced in this area is that there is a common need for attention. Sometimes it is the only way a person knows to gain sympathy and importance. Over the years we have encountered *many* SRA—satanic ritualistic abuse—victims. We have also learned that in most cases the supposed abuse never happened. The individual may *believe* it happened, but generally it is a lie. Now I also think that there are some instances where these really happen, but not nearly to the numbers of people claiming it happened.

We used to see of a lot of these folks. We found limited success and also discovered that there was seldom any evidence to confirm the stories. This became all too common. No names, no addresses, no crime reports, no way to verify any of it. A pastor of a church in a nearby city called me one night. He was distraught. He said, "Don, maybe you can help me. We are at our end in knowing how to deal with a young lady. We have taken her in our home to try to help her. We have tried casting out demons, and it just seems to go on and on—we don't know what to do."

He began to tell me her story, and as he did, I knew I had heard it many times. It's the "SRA story," and I don't want to minimize what may be a very real problem for some. As he told me her story, I said, "The reason you can't help her is because it didn't happen."

There was a silence on the other end of the phone. After a moment he said, "You mean she's lying?" Part of her sad story was that when she stayed at a motel that the church was paying for, her father had busted open the door and brutally raped her. I said, "Take her to the police; I'm betting she won't go."

Again there was silence. Then he said, "You're right. We tried to take her there, but once we arrived, she wouldn't go in." Of course, there are demons involved, but the demons have permission because she continues to believe and perpetuate the lie.

I always seem to end these stories with the same thing. It is truth that enables us to be free. Lies—believing lies—empower the demon.

Chapter 2

INSIGHT INTO
THE DEMONIC REALM

I HAVE A FRIEND, Tommy Thomas, who is a television producer. I meet with him and his beautiful wife, Latrice, a few times a month for Mexican food, which is probably my favorite. Our discussion is generally about what is going on in each of our ministries. On a recent evening I told him I was writing about principalities and powers. He and his wife both encouraged me to check with a man who had been on their TV show, named Howard Pittman. They both agreed that he was one of the most genuine people they had interviewed. "Deeply humble and real," they said.

I spoke with Rev. Pittman a few days ago, and he still holds the excitement of his incredible journey in a near-death experience. He also confirmed what my friends had told me about him, very humble. Back in 1979 Howard Pittman, a Baptist minister for thirty-five years, *died* while on the operating table during surgery and had what we know as a near-death experience (NDE). He has written books about this and his *incredible* journey through the second heaven. A few of his excerpts are indeed interesting.

He says an angel escorted him from his body.

As we moved through that dimension wall into the Second Heaven, I found myself in an entirely different world, far different from anything I had ever imagined. This world was a place occupied by spirit beings as vast in number as the sands of the seashore. These beings were demons [devils], or fallen angels, and were in thousands of different shapes and forms. Even those in similar shapes and forms were contrasted by diverse coloring. Many of the demons were in human shapes or forms and many were in forms similar to animals familiar to our present world. Others were in shapes and forms too hideous to imagine. Some of the forms were so morbid and revolting that I was almost to the point of nausea.[1]

Pittman describes his near-death experience with a sense of awe, yet he says he had some understanding of it.

I did things differently in the spirit realm than what we do here in the physical world. For instance, we did not communicate with our mouths and ears, but rather, we communicated with our minds. It was like projecting our words on thought waves and receiving the answer the same way. Although I could still think to myself without projecting, I discovered that this really did not benefit me because the angels could read my mind.

I could hear different sounds in that world, but I did not hear with my ears. I heard with my mind, but I was still able to hear those sounds. When we traveled, we traveled mostly at what I call the speed of thought. When we traveled at the speed of thought, there was no sensation of movement. The angel would say where we were going and we were there. There were other times when we did not travel in that manner, and I was very much aware of movement while traveling. One of those

times when I was aware of movement was when they
brought me back into the physical world and allowed me
to see the demons working here. We moved about here
somewhat like floating on a cloud. Still, I had the sensation of movement.[2]

Rev. Pittman says the angel guided him through the rank
and file of the structured *second heaven*. That realm he
describes as between the earth and where God lives in the
third heaven. He states:

In the demon world, there is a division of power much
like a military structured chain command with rank
and order. Certain demons carry the title of prince,
which is always the demon in charge of a principality.
A principality is a territory, an area, a place or a group
that may range in size from as large as a nation to as
small as a person. When Satan assigns a prince a task,
the prince is given the authority to act in the name of
Satan and use whatever means necessary or available to
him to accomplish his task.

When we started the tour of the Second Heaven,
the angels began by showing me the different types
of demons. Each demon was revealed to me in a form
that indicated his area of expertise, and I soon discovered that there is no such thing as a general practitioner
in the entire demon world. They have only one area of
expertise which they do very well.[3]

Now, I have not *seen* what Rev. Pittman speaks of, but I
have experienced what he says to be very true. Demons are
not *general practitioners,* but they have very specific duties
and areas of expertise. They are often assigned to specific
areas of the body to do their damage. There are demons, I

believe, for every part of the human body—heart, lungs, kidneys, sexual organs, bones, joints, nerves, and so on. They are assigned by legal permissions that are granted in certain areas. There is authority and power and respect given to higher-ranking demons, and orders are taken and faithfully carried out. I don't know whether it is out of gaining promotions and rewards or out of fear, but I have certainly experienced this reality.

I have also experienced through hundreds of deliverance sessions that demons have many different shapes, forms, and colors—from deceptive beauty to outrageously hideous forms. I have heard many and varied descriptions come from the deliverance candidate. I have documented this from thousands of pages of notes. I have had descriptions of demons given to me by hundreds and hundreds of candidates as they are going through the deliverance process. Virtually always the demon shows himself as a creature of darkness. An octopus is common, serpents of all kinds, scorpions, spiders, leviathans, frogs, dragons, roaches—I have literal pages of demonic descriptions given to me by those who have experienced deliverance. (By the way, *leviathan* is not a demon name; it is a demon form or type.)

I have found that the demons most always organize as a kingdom with leaders calling themselves *princes*. However, the scorpion spirits organize as an army and have military ranks. Proverbs 30:27 gives some strength to this: "The locusts have no king, yet go they forth all of them by bands." The scorpions are generally located in the midsection and virtually always have a function that is fear related, such as anxiety. The ranking spirits in a scorpion army will reveal their status with titles like *general*, *captain*, and, of course, a *commander in chief*. I have found this to be remarkably consistent.

Occasionally they appear to the individual (in the person's mind's eye) as human beings, sometimes with cloaks and dark faces, hooded creatures at other times. These also seem to be somewhat consistent with mental illness of some sort. Sometimes the demons will show themselves as angels, almost to the degree that the person is reluctant to release them. This type of spirit is usually a *false holy spirit* and convinces the person that God is speaking to them directly.

Pittman further states in his recount of traveling through the second heaven that there was a hierarchy revealed to him. He says:

> At the very top of the order were the warring demons which were the cream of Satan's crop. They moved about the Second Heaven and even this present, physical world at will always traveling in groups, never alone. Wherever they went, all other demons moved out of their way. These warring demons were revealed to me in human form. They looked like humans with the exception that they were giants. Appearing to be about eight feet tall, they were rugged and handsomely constructed, somewhat like giant athletes. All of the warring demons were colored bronze. They were giant, bronze soldiers. All of the other demons seemed to be subject to them.
>
> The second most powerful type demon was also revealed to me in human form and these demons looked like ordinary people. All of those possessing this area of expertise seemed to be grouped together at about the second place of command. The third most powerful type and group of demons were revealed to me in mixed shapes and forms. Some had human form while others had half-human and half-animal forms. Others resembled animals in their forms. These demons possessed skills in the dark arts area such as witchcraft and other

related areas. When we got down to the fourth group, or order, all the demons of this rank were revealed in forms other than human. Some had forms like known animals while others had unknown forms. As we moved even further down the order toward the end of the chain of command, all the demons were revealed in horrible and morbid forms. Some were so revolting that their appearance produced nausea. They are so despised by their own companions that they always seem to be lurking off to themselves while in the Second Heaven and even while in this physical world. They do not associate with the other demons except in the line of their duty.[4]

I believe that this man's experience offers some very real insight to the structure of power in the demon world. While I have not seen this with my eyes, as I read his account, it was very similar to what people have described to me during their deliverance sessions. I have gathered information for twenty years about deliverance and the workings of demon powers. While Rev. Pittman's account is not scripture, I do believe that what he relates about his experience is very helpful information to those of us who deal with and have interest in the spirit realm.

I will share later about a friend who was on Tennessee's death row who had an NDE—what he saw as he entered, as an unsaved man, into eternity. He saw and felt things also that are beyond our human experience.

Where Does Satan Live?

Wherein in time past ye walked according to the course of this world, according to the prince of the power of

the air, the spirit that now worketh in the children of
disobedience.

—EPHESIANS 2:2

Since the fall of man, Satan is called the prince or ruler of
the power of the air. That translates literally as *aer*, which is
the atmosphere that surrounds the earth. The word *prince* is
translated from the Greek word *archon* and refers to a ruler,
commander, chief, or leader. Obviously a ruler or commander
would rule over an army. Luke 11:15 tells us that Satan is the
chief ruler and leader of devils. The word for "devils" here is
daimonion, which is literally "a spirit being inferior to God,
superior to men, evil spirits, or the messengers and ministers of the devil." Satan is the principle authority figure that
rules in the earth's atmosphere. That is where the seat of his
authority is located. That is where he *lives* and from whence
he rules. He exercises control and dominion over the hierarchy of demon spirits that oppress mankind.

Some people call this the *second heaven*. Since no one can
know for sure, we can use that terminology. The atmosphere
of our earth becomes thinner and thinner with increasing
altitude and *eases into* what we know as outer space. There
is no definite boundary between the atmosphere and outer
space. Somewhere between sixty to seventy-five miles altitude
we declare it to be outer space. The Kármán line is regarded
as the boundary between atmosphere and outer space.[5] Is the
atmosphere that is around our earth where demons live? Is
Satan's seat of power here? Does he have a house, a palace, a
throne somewhere in the invisible? He roams; he goes to and
fro and up and down in the earth. Doubtless he does have a
seat of power in the atmosphere, but it is a location we could
not possibly know as human beings.

Is there life out there? Of course! Spirits live! Do they live just in the atmosphere? No, I think their domain extends into outer space, but I do not know that with certainty. Where is hell? Satan does not live there, but where is it? Various theories on the location of hell have been put forward. The most common view is that hell is in the center of the earth. Others propose that hell is located in outer space in a black hole. Interesting!

Gerald Thomas[*] is a former inmate who was on Tennessee's death row when he told me:

> Don, I was shot all to pieces, laying in an emergency room in Kingsport, Tennessee. I saw myself rise up out of my body and begin to float toward the ceiling like a ghost. When I turned to look back, I saw my own bloody body and all the people working to save my life. There was some kind of machine pumping air into me, and there were wires attached to my chest and head; they were going to some kind of machine that I later learned was monitoring my heart. I had tubes in my mouth and nose and IVs were all over my body. I was really a mess.
>
> I floated right on through the ceiling and the roof. I could see air conditioner units on the roof and cars on the parking lot under the hospital lights. As I got higher, I could see the street lights of Kingsport and the lights of cars as they moved along the Kingsport streets. I seemed to be moving faster as I got higher. To my right I could see the John B. Dennison Bypass around the city of Kingsport; to my left I could see the Tennessee Eastman Kodak Company. It seemed like it spread all over the city. I have vivid, candid memories of this experience, you know, Don, like it happened yesterday.
>
> At this point it was like something caught me and

---

[*]   Not his real name

just sucked me into space like a vacuum. I was really moving fast, and I couldn't see anything behind me now. I can't describe my feelings, it was happening so fast and, of course, it was something I had never even heard about...you know, an experience like this. I zoomed right past the stars, what a beautiful sight to behold. My mind was filled with wonderment and an inner calm as I passed millions and millions of stars.

I had no concept of time, but apparently all of this happened in a matter of minutes, or maybe even seconds...I was afraid, but I didn't know what to do. Don, when I first shared this, I didn't think anyone would believe me. It really happened, you know I couldn't and wouldn't make up a story like this.[6]

I assured Gerald I believed him and related some similar stories I had encountered with others. However, *all* of the accounts I had been exposed to were from Christians who had "near death," out of the body experiences. Gerald's story is quite the contrary. He said:

In just an instant I was beyond the stars and into a darkness that is indescribable; I could see nothing, not even my hand I placed in front of my eyes. It was sort of a gummy darkness, I mean, it was a darkness that you could feel. A tiny pinpoint of light soon came into view, and soon it began to glow; I was headed straight for it. Then, something strange happened. I started falling, tumbling toward it. The closer I got, I could see it was actually a ball of fire and could even feel the heat from it. The flames leaped and sparks flew from the object; it was like an orange glossy sea of fire.

Don, at that time a terrible odor from the flames became obvious, an awful stench, the most awful smell

I had ever encountered. It was like rotten eggs, a skunk, and the odor of sulfur combined and then ten times worse. As the terrible odor intensified, I could hear hair-raising screams. I snapped...this was people screaming, this odor was that of burning flesh, I was headed to HELL. And, Don, I was almost there.

I remembered that my grandmother had always told me that if I didn't change my ways and quit my fast living that I would wind up in hell someday. I also remembered how I justified my life of violence and crime. I would do like that thief on the cross I had heard about, live like I wanted and just before I died, I would ask God to forgive me. My leather jacket, my "hawkbill" knife, my gun, and my Harley were all I lived for. I thought I was Mr. Bad, and Mr. Bad wasn't afraid of nothing, but he was that night. That night Mr. Bad was afraid! Maybe for the first time in my life, I was frightened.

Don, the heat from the flames was burning me. I did not breathe because of the terrible stench. I tried to shut my eyes, but the sight remained. I didn't know what to do...I prayed, "God, please, please let me go back." I was dangling over the flames of hell. In an instant suddenly I was spinning in reverse away from the flames. I was moving so fast, going back the same route I had come. Back through the awesome stars and back into the view of Kingsport. I was moving so fast, I thought I would surely splatter like a bug on the windshield as the roof of the hospital came into view. But I didn't; I floated very gently down and back into my body.

I remember as I came back through the ceiling, I could see my mother rubbing my arm and my father with his head down praying. My spirit, or soul, just eased right back into my body. I opened my eyes and saw my father. I screamed as loud as I possibly could, "Dad, get me out of here!" I had never been afraid of anything in my life, but now I was scared to death. This experience should have literally scared the *hell* out of me...but it didn't. I was frightened, but I did not change.[7]

(He was saved later while on death row.)

So, is hell in the heart of the earth? In the Old Testament the word translated "hell" is *Sheol*; in the New Testament, it's *Hades* meaning, "unseen," and *Gehenna*, "the Valley of Hinnom." *Sheol* is also translated as "pit" and "grave." Both Sheol and Hades refer to a temporary abode of the dead before judgment (Ps. 9:17; Rev. 1:18). Gehenna refers to an eternal state of punishment for the wicked dead (Mark 9:43). In the New King James Version, Ephesians 4:9 says that before Jesus ascended into heaven, "He also first descended into the lower parts of the earth." Some Christians take "the lower parts of the earth" as a reference to hell, where they say Jesus spent the time between His death and resurrection. However, other translations give a different view, indicating that Jesus came to earth. This view says it's a reference to His incarnation, not to His location after death.

The notion that hell is somewhere in outer space, possibly in a black hole, is based on the knowledge that black holes are places of great heat and pressure from which nothing, not even light, can escape. Read again the account of Gerald's description of the darkness.

The *outer darkness* is a place referred to three times in the King James Version in the Gospel of Matthew into which a person may be "cast" and where there is "weeping and gnashing of teeth" (Matt. 8:12; 22:13; 25:30). It is interesting that Jesus chose this term. Many believe that the outer darkness is hell; however, there are some who associate the outer darkness more generally as a place of separation from God.

According to scientists the center of the earth is not a nice place to visit, unless you like hanging out in a blast furnace. The outer core of the earth, about two-thirds of the way to the center, is molten iron. The temperature is believed to exceed 11,000 degrees Fahrenheit, hotter than the surface of the sun. The deepest drill hole man has accomplished is only eight to ten miles deep. To reach the center of the earth you would need to drill nearly four thousand miles.[8]

Scripture does not give us a geological or cosmological location of hell. But we know that it is a literal place of real torment. Hell may have a physical location in this universe, or it may be in an entirely different *dimension*. Whatever the case, the location of hell is far less important than the need to avoid going there.

Look at the parable Jesus used to describe hell:

> There was a certain rich man who was clothed in purple and fine linen and fared sumptuously every day. But there was a certain beggar named Lazarus, full of sores, who was laid at his gate, desiring to be fed with the crumbs which fell from the rich man's table. Moreover the dogs came and licked his sores. So it was that the beggar died, and was carried by the angels to Abraham's bosom. The rich man also died and was buried. And being in torments in Hades, he lifted up his eyes and saw Abraham afar off, and Lazarus in his bosom. Then he cried and said, "Father Abraham, have mercy on me, and send Lazarus that he may dip the tip of his finger in water and cool my tongue; for I am tormented in this flame." But Abraham said, "Son, remember that in your lifetime you received your good things, and likewise Lazarus evil things; but now he is comforted and you are tormented. And besides all this, between us and you

there is a great gulf fixed, so that those who want to pass from here to you cannot, nor can those from there pass to us." Then he said, "I beg you therefore, father, that you would send him to my father's house, for I have five brothers, that he may testify to them, lest they also come to this place of torment." Abraham said to him, "They have Moses and the prophets; let them hear them." And he said, "No, father Abraham; but if one goes to them from the dead, they will repent." But he said to him, "If they do not hear Moses and the prophets, neither will they be persuaded though one rise from the dead."

—LUKE 16:19–31, NKJV

Note some interesting truths from this parable. The rich man, the unsaved man, had all of his five senses in hell. He could see, hear, smell, touch, and taste. He could also evaluate and feel concern.

Several years ago I preached a message about the reality of hell. A doctor and his wife had been attending the church for several Sundays. I had been to this doctor as a patient; he was a general practitioner and was a very nice man; however, by his own words, he was not a believer. I could tell that he was very uncomfortable during the message, but he did not come at the altar call. I went to one of the doors to shake hands and speak with the people as they left. As this doctor came by, he took my hand and with a sheepish grin said, "You almost got me today, preacher, you almost got me."

A couple of years later I was shocked to read in the paper that this doctor had died at a very young age. I hope he made a decision to receive Christ before he died.

The Book of Job records a conversation between God and Satan. God asks what Satan has been doing, and he responded:

"From going to and fro in the earth, and from walking up and down in it" (Job 1:7).

Not just walking to and fro on the earth, but "walking up and down in it." Hmm...walking "up and down."

Jesus made a striking statement about the authority of Satan in John 12:31: "Now is the judgment of this world; now shall the prince of this world be cast out." Jesus said again, in John 14:30, "Hereafter I will not talk much with you; for the prince of this world cometh, and hath nothing in me." Jesus clearly taught that Satan is the god of *this* world and even more clearly said in John 3:16 that God so loved "this" world that He gave His only begotten Son that "this" world might be saved.

The Word of God teaches that Satan is the prince or the ruler of this world, this present world order, which includes the systems and governments of mankind and the present condition of human affairs. He is the commander and chief, exercising authority over the rulers of the darkness of this world, which includes principalities, powers, authorities, and every wicked spirit.

Paul also declared that Satan exercises authority as the god of this world in 2 Corinthians 4:4: "In whom the god of this world hath blinded the minds of them which believe not, lest the light of the glorious gospel of Christ, who is the image of God, should shine unto them." Scripture reveals that Jesus Christ and the apostle Paul clearly taught that Satan is the god and ruler of this present world. This is why the world is in such a mess. But God had a plan that included exalting Christ above all principalities and authority.

This is very difficult to grasp since we are talking about an invisible kingdom.

Think with me...if you were the devil, how would you organize your countless numbers of fallen angels? Since he is not able to be everywhere present at all times, he must be in a place of rule where he delegates his authority and his wishes to be carried out. Imagine yourself in this dark but lofty position of evil. You are "god of the earth," and you are aware that there are seven billion or more human beings on the earth. Do you think you would form a *cabinet* of the most brilliant and most powerful of the demons? How many levels of government would you need? Remember you are "warring against the saints"; you are opposing the work of God.

I'm thinking I might start with at least one demon for each of the seven continents. These would have to be the best. I would see to it that those seven chose demons under them to rule various areas of these continents; they would be principalities. After the regions are established, I would also make lesser principalities for specific regions in these territories. For instance, in the United States it would be very similar to the governmental structure we have in place. One powerful demon ruling with many advisors and cabinet members, and then those that rule divisional or regional areas of the country, one over particular states, one over certain counties, one over county seat cities and local towns. Each of these rulers would have a large government of its own to manage the affairs of darkness—one over communities and neighborhoods, blocks of the streets, certain houses. There would be multitudes of workers in the vast kingdom of darkness.

There would be so many in this governmental structure of evil that special appointees would be given territories over waters, mountains, deserts, trees, barren remote areas— covering all the earth. By the way, I have encountered demon powers who describe their territories and responsibilities in such terms. For instance, I know the prince of Texas and many of his subordinates. I have encountered many principalities of certain counties and cities and many of their underlings. I know the prince of many states and regions in the world. They show up, and under oath before Jehovah God they reveal their territories. I have encountered hundreds of territorial spirits; I have recorded their names and geographical areas. I don't fight with them; they come to protect their kingdom on the inside of the individual. I do not have authority to cast them down, or else I would do so for the entire world. I do, however, command them to return to the heavenly realm and to not interfere with the individual's deliverance. They always obey.

How many demons are working in this vast network of evil against God and God's people? Billions? Thousands of thousands? Remembering that they are spirits, I don't suppose there is any value in speculating. Demon powers that are in or attached to people are minions of higher-ranking spirits. These we can and do cast into the abyss. I have found that they can split, divide, multiply, fragment, clone, and use various other ways of deceiving and evading the deliverance process. I always forbid them from doing this in my commands to demon powers. I also have found that these spirit beings have the ability to make decisions. Many of them seem to have, for lack of a better description, *brat* personalities. They communicate with other demons and actually call for help to those in higher rank.

Demons are not disembodied spirits looking for a home. Many ministries say something to that effect. Demons never had a body. I have found the demon powers are, without doubt, fallen angels, which in every way possible oppose the work of God. They are not drifters or floaters without purpose. They are sent by higher-ranking spirits to do the most damage possible to the kingdom of God. When open doors, entry ways, are recognized in the lives of God's people, they can enter into human beings and oppress them. They enter into the soulish area of man, not the spirit. They are tormentors above all, liars with mastery in deception. They absolutely are not the spirits of dead people.

There are multitudes of inexplicable stories of *haunted* places. There are times that I have *felt* the oppressing presence of demonic spirits in certain places. The phenomenon can be nothing but demon powers. Departed spirits of humans cannot linger or return with some kind of duty or unfulfilled mission. To be absent from this body is to be present with the Lord or to be in hell. Note the parable of the rich man and the beggar Lazarus (Luke 16:19–31). Lazarus died and was carried by the angels to heaven. The rich man died, was buried and in hell. Both men were still very much alive in eternity. There is a great impassable gulf fixed that prevents return to this earth. There is only one scriptural possibility for haunting— demons! It can be nothing but deceptive actions of demons. As I stated, demons are not *disembodied* spirits; they never had a body.

You wonder how a demon spirit can enter a follower of Christ. Look at the apparent ease with which Satan entered into Judas. John 13:27 records: "As soon as Judas took the bread, Satan entered into him. 'What you are about to do, do quickly,' Jesus told him" (NIV). The prince of darkness did personal battle with Jesus, and he used people to try to attain victory. He "entered" into Judas. Demons enter people today, and their goal is still the same—to war against us, to oppose everything of God. We can best understand this by knowing that it is not Satan himself that we deal with, but his legions of demon powers on assignment from his kingdom of darkness. Jesus said to cast them *out*—so they must be *in*.

It is the foot soldier demons that get into the lives of people. People are demonized by evil spirits who are under the rule of higher-ranking spirits. When the demon on the inside of a person is confronted, he most likely represents a higher-ranking demon power in the heavenlies; most often he uses the name of that demon.

When permission is given—that is, the granting of legal rights, whether through ancestral transgressions or open doors of trauma, abuse, disobedience, and unconfessed sin—demons can enter the believer. This is demonization; it is spiritual oppression. The spirits dwell in the flesh and/or the soul but never in the spirit, for that is where the Holy Spirit lives.

While the unclean spirits may possess an area of a person's life, genuine possession by demons cannot happen to a Christian, for possession is ownership, and we are owned by the Lord Jesus. Remember, we are purchased, bought with a price!

Perhaps the most easily understood comparison is that of the tabernacle or temple. The Bible often refers to us as a tabernacle and as the temple of God. First Corinthians 3:16–17 says this: "Know ye not that ye are the temple of God, and that the Spirit of God dwelleth in you? If any man defile the temple of God, him shall God destroy; for the temple of God is holy, which temple ye are."

Remember the tabernacle as three distinct parts:

1. The outer court

2. The holy place

3. The holy of holies

Compare this to the human tabernacle.

1. The flesh

2. The soul

3. The spirit

As no unclean thing could enter the holy of holies, so no unclean thing can enter the spirit of a believer. The unclean spirits enter or attach themselves to the flesh and/or the soul of a man. Paul refers to our body as our "earthly tabernacle" in 2 Corinthians 5:1.

Chapter 3

THE DEMONS' FAVORITE SCRIPTURE

D ON'T BE SURPRISED that demons know Scripture; not only do they know it, but they also know how to twist it! What I am about to say is not revolutionary revelation, but it certainly opened my eyes as a key truth to deliverance ministry and to walking in freedom. This is something you must know to effectively deal with the kingdom of darkness! It concerns the *demons' favorite scripture*: Matthew 12:43–45. This scripture puzzled me, and for months I could not reconcile this with other scripture. I had to stop working on the book *When Pigs Move In* because these verses made no sense to me. Why cast them out if they can come back stronger? I asked for weeks for the Holy Spirit to enlighten me and show me truth.

Actually this information is perhaps the most important I can share with those interested in deliverance ministry. Get this phrase locked in your mind: "Gone out or cast out." It is a key to ministering in truth. I had heard, all my life, preachers making reference to this verse and teaching that the demons can come back unless the house is filled with the Holy Spirit, faithful Bible reading, worship, prayers, and giving: "You have to fill the house…" That is not even implied here.

> When the unclean spirit is gone out of a man, he
> walketh through dry places, seeking rest, and findeth
> none. Then he saith, I will return into my house from
> whence I came out; and when he is come, he findeth it
> empty, swept, and garnished. Then goeth he, and taketh
> with himself seven other spirits more wicked than him-
> self, and they enter in and dwell there: and the last state
> of that man is worse than the first. Even so shall it be
> also unto this wicked generation.
>
> —MATTHEW 12:43-45

In Matthew 12 Jesus reproved the Pharisees and the generation of Israel to which He came. He healed and cast out
demons. He rebuked them for their unbelief and likened the
nation to one who has demons. He spoke of them as a generation that were resolved to continue in the possession and
under the power of Satan, in spite of all of God's attempts to
rescue them and free them. Jesus uses a parable to compare
them to one out of whom the devil is gone but returns with
double force. The devil is here called *the unclean spirit.*

The parable represents Satan and his demons possessing
men's bodies. Matthew Henry says: "Christ having lately cast
out a devil, and they having said he had a devil, gave occasion
to show how much they were under the power of Satan. This is
a further proof that Christ did not cast out devils by compact
with the devil, for then he [demon] would soon have returned
again; but Christ's ejectment of him was final, and such as
barred a reentry: we find him charging the evil spirit to go out,
and enter no more, Mark 9:25."[1]

What a great statement; there was no deal with Satan as the
Jews had accused Him. There are two key issues in clarifying
this horribly misused scripture:

1. It was a parable.

2. The word is *gone* out, not *cast* out. I will say that again: "gone out," not "cast out"!

Another great insight from Matthew Henry reads:

> Probably the devil was wont sometimes thus to sport with those he had possession of; he would go out, and then return again with more fury; hence the lucid intervals of those in that condition were commonly followed with the more violent fits. When the devil is gone out, he is uneasy, for he sleeps not except he have done mischief (Prov. 4:16); he walks in dry places, like one that is very melancholy; he seeks rest but finds none, till he returns again. When Christ cast the legion out of the man, they begged leave to enter into the swine, where they went not long in dry places, but into the lake presently.
>
> The application of the parable makes it to represent the case of the body of the Jewish church and nation: So shall it be with this wicked generation, that now resist, and will finally reject, the gospel of Christ...and then he shall take a durable possession here, and the state of this people is likely to be more desperately damnable...than it was before Christ came among them, or would have been if Satan had never been cast out.[2]

Clearly Jesus makes this statement in the parable in regard to what He called "a wicked generation."

I have been doing this for a few years! Virtually all believers who have a casual knowledge of Scripture misunderstand and misapply the scripture here. This is what they say: "If you don't keep the house filled, then the cast-out demons will come back seven times stronger." That is NOT true! That is not what is being taught here. If, as most believe, demons can return in double force once they have been cast out, wouldn't it be unwise to cast them out? What would allow demons to do this? To be cast out and yet later return?

Nonsense; look carefully at the scripture parable Jesus used. The demons here are not cast out, they are *gone* out—apparently they leave to try to find a better home, knowing they can return because there is still an open door. When the demons decided to return, it was not because the house had not been filled (so often and erroneously taught). The house was in good shape, it was garnished, clean, and decorated. The demons knew they could go back because they knew they still had legal permission. Their legal rights to be there had never been canceled.

When demons are cast out in the name of Jesus, there is finality. Those particular demons cannot return! However, there are plenty of demons who can and possibly will enter if legal rights are granted. That an individual can continue a downward spiral is true. Whether an individual goes through deliverance or not, if he grants them opportunity, other demons can enter. It is so important to know this. Demons love to intimidate deliverance candidates with lies and threats.

Never do we command demons to go into "dry places," which seems to be where they congregate and make their plans and evil strategies. Demons have done a good job at using these scriptures to confuse and prevent people from seeking deliverance. I have had many people ask me, "Now what do I do to keep them from coming back seven times stronger?" Most preachers even make misleading comments about this section of Scripture. You have heard words like, "Be sure and keep the house filled so the demons don't come back stronger."

The demons love it. Keeping people in ignorance and fear is their specialty. In many, many years of ministry I have never seen this happen—someone being worse off because they experienced deliverance—never! However, someone who continues in a lifestyle that initially granted permission will be once again entangled, because doors stay open. There is a big difference! Don't be intimidated by confusion and lies; the demons cannot come back stronger because those same demons cannot come back.

When I leave my office, I *go out* knowing I can come back and could even invite some friends to come back with me. I have a door; I have the keys. However, if the owner of the building evicts me, takes the keys back, and demands that I leave, I can't come back. Big difference—*gone* out and *cast* out. Leaving of your own volition is very different than being kicked out!

Read again Matthew Henry's comment on this:

> Christ did not cast out devils by compact with the devil, for then he [demon] would soon have returned again; but Christ's ejectment of him was final, and such as barred a reentry: we find him charging the evil spirit to *go out, and enter no more,* Mark 9:25.[3]

The commands we give when *casting* out demons is that they go into the abyss, the pit of hell, and never return again. That does not mean that the individual cannot continue to live a dysfunctional lifestyle by being disobedient to God. Some do make choices to disobey and to grant legal rights to demons. Choices always remain, and bad choices generally open doors to other demons. Don't give them too much credit. Don't fear them, and don't let them gain an advantage by misuse of God's Holy Word!

Someone remarked to me recently that they were told by others in a Bible study group that it is not wise to venture into deliverance ministry. They said, "We were told that we must have a huge prayer covering before attempting deliverance." Interesting!

Where does it say that? Of course, I would always prefer to have many people praying for me, but the disciples didn't have that covering—they had a commission. Jesus sent them to people. He sent the twelve disciples and He sent seventy *rookie* disciples out, and there was no large prayer covering; they went in Jesus's name, and that has not changed today. The name of Jesus is sufficient.

Beyond this, the minister's life must be usable; you can't act in Jesus's authority unless that authority has first been exercised in your own life. You can't cast from others what you entertain yourself. But at the same time, I say with great boldness, know who you are in Christ. Know what has been given to you in Christ. Take everything that is yours! We are heirs of God and joint heirs with Jesus Christ!

Do you think the demons have their own language? Do they have a unique method of communicating? I have been doing deliverance a long time. I have heard through many candidates for deliverance descriptions of creatures beyond their abilities to explain. They often describe grotesque creatures of darkness. I have also heard, many times, the demonic powers speak in other tongues with anger and hatred directed at me. As a matter of fact, if you removed the emotion of anger and hatred from the tongue, it sounds much like the tongues that I have heard in some churches through the years.

So do they have their own language? The obvious answer is no. They seem to understand English very well. They obey commands given them in the name of Jesus, regardless of the language. But do they have a unique method of communication? Absolutely; they have an ability to share and exchange their information in ways far beyond ours—most likely mind to mind. Even though we discover more and better ways to communicate almost daily, we are far behind what goes on in the spirit world.

I suppose one way to understand their methods is to say that they have a vast network and communication system that is maybe similar to ours. Maybe we can understand their method of transmitting information similar to the way I understand our satellite systems that bounce information from one point to another. I really don't understand it; I just know that it works. It amazes me to think that I can click a couple of buttons and instantly message someone in another part of the world. We can send not only words of communication but also pictures and live videos, all transmitted in a system that involves invisible waves in the atmosphere.

I believe the spirit world communicates not only with their minds, one to another, but also *to our minds*. We are recipients of evil thoughts and images sent to us by demon powers. We are spirits that have a soul that lives in a body. First and foremost, we are spirits. That we can receive these messages, or *temptations*, as Jesus called them, should not surprise us. That we can also receive inspiration, that we can resist or receive by choice, is a given.

Demon spirits that gain access to a believer likely live inside that person in the various areas of the *soul*. The body and/or the soul is where demon spirits can live, but not in the spirit. They get access by unconfessed sin or generational permissions in the ancestry, or by a variety of other consents. "But if our gospel be hid, it is hid to them that are lost: In whom the god of this world hath blinded the minds of them which believe not, lest the light of the glorious gospel of Christ, who is the image of God, should shine unto them" (2 Cor. 4:3–4).

The soul includes our mind, will, and emotions. I'm not really certain how anybody knows this for sure, but it probably includes our memory and personality. The mind is the most probable place for demon spirits. They may also attach themselves to individuals. This is demonic oppression. Now, how do they communicate?

Virtually every demon power within a person has a territorial spirit in the heavenly realm or in the atmosphere. The demons on the inside are like a cell, or a seed, from the territorial demon. Casting out this demon on the inside and into the abyss only weakens the territorial spirit; it cancels his rights to the individual. However, he remains active in the heavenly realm.

I have found that the *inside demons* want to return to the heavenly realm for reassignment, but never do we allow this. The demons in the atmosphere *run their inside kingdom* by *remote control.* Territorial spirits cannot be cast into the abyss; else we could just do it and be through with them. We can destroy the works of the demons, which the Bible says Jesus came to do. However, we cannot destroy the demonic realm in the heavenly realm. If He came to destroy the devil himself, we would not be dealing with this. He came to destroy *their works,* and when He comes again, He will destroy Satan himself. "For this purpose the Son of God was manifested, that he might destroy the works of the devil" (1 John 3:8). Right now we are destroying his works.

While it seems clear that demons communicate with each other *mind to mind,* I believe an easy way to understand their work in our minds is through the word *transmit*; that is, they are able to send messages and thoughts to our mind. Our brain has an amazing capacity to receive, record, and recover thoughts. Our *mind* seems to be separate and in the *soulish* area. When someone says, "Well, that's just in their mind," that is exactly where a demon would choose to be.

There is typically more than one demon on the inside, usually many more. Maybe seven kingdoms would be an average. Each of these kingdoms will have many other demons that work in this kingdom, all with various related assignments. For instance, you might have seven kingdoms with numbers of demons in each kingdom, kind of like a corporation would organize with various departments and workers.

I will give an example. The demon power Apollyon, which I have encountered hundreds of times, is a high-ranking spirit; his demon powers have entered into many people, virtually always with the function of fear. Revelation 9:11 states, "And they had a king over them, which is the angel of the bottomless pit, whose name in the Hebrew tongue is Abaddon, but in the Greek tongue hath his name Apollyon."

The demon powers in his kingdom virtually always have a fear-related function. It may be anxiety, panic, depression, hopelessness, suicide, and/or a variety of other assignments in that area. Each of these demonic functions is carried out by separate demons that have individual names—but they always have a leader in superior rank. I believe when doorways are opened, it's like a demon sending a live video image to the heavenly realm, and demons scramble to gain entrance to the person.

Imagine cameras mounted in every area where it is possible for you to be, like eyes in the sky watching and looking for opportunities. While it is certain the demons are looking, how much more are the angels looking for opportunities to bless.

Remember that the function of all demon powers is to steal, kill, and destroy. The demon power *Apollyon* claims to be a destroyer. I actually encountered this demon power in a deliverance session recently. I met with a medical doctor from New England; he is very successful and very brilliant, but he was tormented with demons. He was saved in medical school but had experienced many rejections and disappointments in his life. The initial opening in his life was from ancestral permission on his mother's side of the family.

This doctor was tormented with suicidal thoughts, hatred for some of the people who had hurt him, fears of tomorrow, and among many others things, insomnia. The territorial spirit over this man's demonic kingdom was *Apollyon*. There were many demon powers in this kingdom of torment. They boasted and defied me at first, until they were reminded that it is not me with whom they were dealing, but Jesus Christ.

This man with doctorate degrees and years of medical practice experienced the demons lying to him and trying to harm him during the session. He told me afterward that the lies and extreme insomnia started after he made a commitment to come here for deliverance. They all left. They all obeyed in Jesus's name and left when commanded to leave. The doctor said, "I knew it, I knew it." He also told me that medicines had done nothing to help his symptoms, but now he felt great peace.

Demons have a unique ability to know about our lives and our plans. The doctor told me, "From the moment I started to fill out the request form to come see you, they started. Even after I arrived here, they kept lying to me: 'You don't need this. You're a doctor…just deal with it; you know it's not demons.'" He said the lies continued right up to our prayer prior to the session and during the deliverance. "I knew what it was," he said.

Many, many times people have told me that as soon as they start to investigate being free, the demons start their lies. I know demons can read and understand our communications, but the thing is, they tremble at the name of Jesus!

Demon Names and Characteristics

I had only been doing deliverance a short time when I encountered what seemed to be a most unusual situation. I was scheduled to preach in the chapel services at a women's prison in central Texas. I had been there many times and had preached some about Jesus's work in the area of deliverance. The chaplain at the prison asked if I could come early on a specific date and meet with eight different women who had requested deliverance sessions. These would be done in an office adjacent to his. I agreed. I knew very little about the deliverance process at the time.

After a couple of deliverance sessions that were somewhat typical, the third female inmate came for her session. After we had prayed and canceled all legal permissions, she began to tell me something about her life. "I have never told anyone this," she said, "not anyone. Not my closest friend, not a doctor or counselor...no one!" She then began to tell me about a visitor she often experienced at night. The tone of her voice was to make certain I believed her. She said, "This *thing*, for lack of a better word, appears at the foot of my bed. It's like a mist or a fog, but it is in a human form. I don't care what anybody says; that thing lays on me and has sex with me!" She said, "It is real, and I know it is a demon."

I knew also that it was a demon, but I had certainly never encountered anything like that. That was my first experience with the incubus spirit. Since then I have dealt with it many, many times.

I remember that after I returned home, I called my friend

Frank Hammond, who lived in Plainview, Texas. I explained what I had encountered. He said, "Oh, you have met the incubus demon. You will deal with that demon many times in your deliverance ministry." He was correct; we run into that a lot.

Now suppose that was happening to you. Whom would you tell? Do you think your pastor would understand? Likely not! I want to share a little about some of the demons we encounter on a regular basis. Stories and writings have long existed about this demon. It was in the eighteenth century that physicians began to suggest that *incubi* were only the result of the human imagination, and as a result a lot of the hype about it died down. This is pretty much the explanation given by psychologists today. They will say it is a figment of one's imagination. It is only in the mind. Think about that a minute—only in the mind. That's exactly where demons want to be—*in* the mind. Funny thing about that, when the demon is cast out, it doesn't happen anymore.

There is a similar demon that sexually torments males. This demon is called a *succubus*. *Succubi* are the female version of *incubi*, although the word is actually masculine in Medieval Latin, because demons are supposedly sexless. The feminine form is *succuba*.

There are many such demons that are similar in purpose with perversion and fantasy lust being their primary functions. The incubus and succubus are not names of demon spirits; they are types, but each one will have an individual name.

I have perhaps fifty thousand names of demons spirits with whom we have had personal dealings. I want to give you an idea how this works by sharing accounts of a few. In many of our deliverance sessions we find clusters of demons in particular locations in the body, which have similar functions. One example is that we find the demon *Molech* or *Moloch*, which is virtually always located in or about the female organs of a woman, and is usually there by permission of abortion or sexual abuse. Of course, this could even be from an ancestral curse by those who gave permissions in previous generations.

When there are disorders in the female organs, we find not only *Molech* but also *Belial, Elizabeth, Sedona,* and others. They seem to always be together. *Sedona* claims to be *Belial's* twin. There are many others; this is only an example.

Another example is the area of *false gifts*. There are several demons who are common in this area. The *false gifts* spirits are demons that we encounter very often. They include *Baphomet, Beelzebub, Orion, Galendo, Sentar,* and *Sawyer*—these are demon powers—and many others who are virtually always involved in deception and imitation of Spirit gifts. This information would be helpful to any genuine minister of deliverance.

I remember a lady telling me that she caused a big split in her church in California. She said, "I had just begged the Holy Spirit to give me a prophetic gift." Then one day it happened; she started giving "words from God" to people. She told me her pastor had talked to her about it and told her that what she was doing was out of line. She did not yield to his advice or correction. She told me, "After all, I was hearing from God." She continued, "I hurt so many lives and created so much confusion and dissension that I eventually left the church broken and ashamed. It all seemed so real at the time." Now this lady warns about the deception and how easily Christians can be fooled by what is planted in their minds and *seems* to be from God. "The fruit," she said, "is rotten."

There are demons that have unique and special assignments

to virtually every part of the human body. You name an organ, and there is a *family* of demons that work in that area. It's almost as if they were unionized and don't cross over picket lines. Let's choose an organ of the body, for example, the kidneys. *Akeem, Anoch, Apollyon, Barak,* and *Pentoulle* are five names of the more than thirty that we have encountered to have a function of kidney disorders.

While this of course is not science, it is pretty reliable information in the deliverance world. After many, many years and thousands of deliverance sessions with people from all walks of life, I have pages of consistent notes. No one could talk me out of this being real! I know it is.

While thinking in this line of demonic functions and categories, you might wonder which kingdoms we encounter most often. You likely won't be surprised to know it is the kingdoms of fear, anger, and rejection. We have recorded huge kingdoms with pages and pages of demonic names. Remember, you cannot cast out demons against someone's will or until all legal permissions have been canceled. Never try this. I will not list names in these kingdoms, but I assure you, there is virtually an unlimited number.

It is not wise to go around saying a demon's name or to think about them too much—only when the need for deliverance arises and a person has come to you for help. Don't seek them out, and don't become a demon diagnostician. Focus on Jesus and His Holy Word.

I recall a few years ago having services in several prisons in the Texas Panhandle. Pampa, Amarillo, Dalhart, and Tulia were the cities where these prisons are located. There are two in Pampa and two in Amarillo. From the time my wife dropped me off at the DFW airport until I arrived back home several days later I was harassed by demon spirits. I won't go into the details; it might need to be a separate book. After preaching for three days in the prisons, I had my final service in Tulia. In spite of all the opposition, many men were saved, and there was a strong anointing.

During the service at the Tulia transfer unit, one of the Hispanic brothers seated in the back seemed to be *locked* in on me as I preached. When the service was over and men were going back to the assigned areas, this man came to me and shook my hand. He said, "Brother, the Holy Spirit told me to tell you something. I don't know what it means." He then said, "He said to tell you that Satan has assigned a high-ranking spirit to you. Do you know what that means?" I told him that I did know, and he said he would continue to pray for me.

I remember walking down the halls of that prison toward the front door. There was a huge clap of thunder, and the officer at the door asked which direction I was headed. I told him Amarillo, and he said, "Sir, be careful; we just got word there is a tornado on the ground between here and there." In my spirit I was hearing a calm assurance: "Same authority, same authority!"

Many times I wonder, "Why do the demons do what they do? Are they rewarded for their work?" Logically I would guess it is promotion within the ranks, but also satisfaction in their evil work against God's people. Demons are intrinsically evil. They can be nothing else. While it is their nature to do evil and carry out Satan's assignments, I'm sure their methodology adapts to current situations.

Do you suppose that demonic strategy was changed after the resurrection? How many demons do you think participated in the plot to murder Jesus? All of them! You see, they thought they would win. I believe that to some extent they still believe that. I have heard in deliverance sessions from the mouth of the candidate, "They are saying, 'We will win.'"

I am assuming that for four thousand years they tried to prevent the birth of Jesus and failed. They tried to kill Him and eliminate Him and failed. Do you think the strategy has changed?

Does Satan know his end and still refuses to quit? He was spoken to in the Garden of Eden by God Himself. He didn't just read about the prophecy; he was the direct recipient of it! As a constant reminder serpents are still crawling on their bellies. The truth of Genesis 3:14–15 is still alive and active, and Satan is very aware of it:

> And the LORD God said unto the serpent, Because thou hast done this, thou art cursed above all cattle, and above every beast of the field; upon thy belly shalt thou go, and dust shalt thou eat all the days of thy life: And I will put enmity between thee and the woman, and between thy seed and her seed; it shall bruise thy head, and thou shalt bruise his heel.

Deceiving people with their clever lies is still the method of operation. They have had to alter their deception, as man has advanced in knowledge and technology. For instance, in America people will not bow before an idol of Molech and sacrifice their babies. Molech worship is an abomination unto the Lord, which originated from the Ammonites. One of the rituals connected to Molech worship is the sacrificing of children unto the Ammonite god Molech, as an expression of their devotion to him. It is interesting that the Ammonites descended from the incestuous acts of Lot and his daughters. Demons rejoiced at this opportunity, and demon powers Ammon and Moab still are active in lust and perversion.

We would never do as these foolish idol worshippers. When Israel fell into idolatry, which sadly happened many times in their national history, one of the gods they worshipped was Molech, and thus they offered up their sons and daughters as human sacrifices to it. Such a practice is an utter abomination unto the Lord.

Molech is still a baby killer! Today he is worshipped in the world through abortion. We have advanced too much to *pass through the fire*—to take a child and sacrifice it on a fiery altar. So apparently Molech and other demon powers have changed their strategy.

Many of the pagan practices and rituals of the various demon powers that were worshipped are still practiced today in a different guise. Many of the secret societal organizations through their pledges and ancient oaths and vows still call on the demons to help them. They speak the names of demons in the private rituals and are led to believe they hold secrets of power and control.

Still the same lies, and the demons receive worship by a means that is now accepted and sought after. You would not believe the number of people who go through deliverance and find that some of the oaths and vows taken, and pledges and ceremonies participated in by an ancestor, or even perhaps by them, have granted permission for demon powers in their lives! The names of the demons we encounter through these secret society organizations (fraternities and sororities) are remarkably consistent. These demon powers are the same that sought worship through the sun, moon, rivers, and so forth by their ancients. My point is that the demons have adapted to our *advancement*, and their strategy has changed somewhat.

But what about the change that took place during the death, burial, and resurrection? Four thousand years of demonic effort to stop the birth of Christ failed, and the intense effort to eliminate Him through death has now failed. Do you think there might have been an emergency meeting at Satan's house on Monday after Resurrection Sunday?

I can see it now, all of the top demons called in. The partying had stopped, and what looked like a giant demonic win now called for an urgent change of plans. Their attempt to destroy Israel would continue, but now it's more complicated. The Savior, Wonderful Counselor, Mighty God, was alive. He had conquered death; he took the sting out of it. The grave could no longer be used to bring terror. He had promised to send power to new believers. He had commissioned them to heal the sick and cast out demons. He had given them authority in His name.

Satan knew something was coming; he knew Jesus had promised to send the Holy Spirit. He knows Bible prophecy. But now it's not just the nation of Israel that he is trying to destroy. He must deal with a host of Gentile believers. The body of Christ would have to be dealt with. The written Word of God would become a major influence in the world. Do you suppose the demonic world has meetings and strategy sessions? I believe there was scrambling and high-level meetings taking place when Jesus stepped out of the tomb and the grave could not hold Him.

I can hear the demons screaming in agony as the living Lord Jesus rose from the dead. The call for high-level powers made its way through the atmosphere. Satan must have trembled yet cried out in anger. Now there's a new problem. Clever attacks on key individuals must happen: Kill the apostles. Stop the message. Persecute. Bring physical harm and murder to the purveyors of the gospel.

I believe there are strategy sessions on a regular basis in the kingdom of darkness. Even when a believer receives deliverance and news reaches the territorial spirits in the heavenly realm, I feel certain they are discussing things like, "What worked before? How did we gain entrance to that life initially? Let's try it again; let's do something similar and see how they respond." New demons are assigned. None of the demons are omnipotent or omnipresent, including Satan. Omniscience is not a characteristic of any demon power, and of course, they are incapable of being immutable; they are the opposite.

While their tactics always include steal, kill, and destroy, they must adapt to various situations. When Jesus made it possible for anyone to be saved, great attention had to be given to prevent the world from knowing this. When people did believe and receive Christ, great effort had to be given to keep the new believers in a measure of darkness. Satan knew what Jesus could do; he knew His miracle-working power. What he didn't know is what Jesus could do through a believer.

He knew he no longer held the keys of death, hell, and the grave. Jesus took them from him and declared, "I am he that liveth, and was dead; and, behold, I am alive for evermore, Amen; and have the keys of hell and of death" (Rev. 1:18). He knows he can do nothing to prevent the power and authority that Jesus gives from being real; he can only do something to keep man from knowing and acting upon it.

I'm pretty sure discussion was made about the *little Jesus* they would be dealing with. Previously they had one Jesus with which to contend; now there will be thousands and millions who carry His authority. The Holy Spirit began to live in each new believer. He teaches, guides, comforts, walks beside, and empowers believers as they learn to listen to Him and live according to God's Word. The demons must be diligent. I feel certain this was discussed at the emergency meeting. Satan must have been exhorting his strongest demons with fervor. He was asserting, "We must prevent man from believing, and we must prevent believers from exercising their rights in Christ."

The purpose will remain the same, just different and updated tactics and constant relevant updates on strategy. The "updates" must go out in the demonic realm more often than they do on our computers. They must constantly search for new and updated ways to instill doubt and unbelief. I once preached a message called, "The Sin Most Often Committed by Women." Yes, it received a lot of attention. The answer should not surprise you, though; it is also the sin most often committed by men. It is unbelief! That has always been Satan's method—instill doubt about what God says and who God is.

My mother was tormented all of my adult life. I don't know how many doctors she may have seen; it seemed to all start with a hysterectomy. I'm not certain there is a connection spiritually, but I suspect it. I was just married and only twenty. She became more and more nervous and anxious about things and life in general. In a few words, she just couldn't seem to cope with anything. My dad came to me one day and told me she was being admitted to a psychiatric hospital in Dallas.

Not only was my dad greatly concerned about her, but he was also troubled about the cost. We never had much money, and this would be very expensive. After a few weeks she was released with a diagnosis of paranoid schizophrenia. She was troubled the rest of her life.

This included shock treatments and dozens of hospital stays. My dad would sit in the hospitals with her for hours. I don't know how he did it. He spent virtually his last dime on doctors and medicine; there were few days of normalcy.

At the time I didn't have any knowledge or experience with

demon powers. My mom was tormented, and as a result, my dad lived under much stress. I recall on one of my mom's last hospital stays, doctors told us she would need to be transported to a psychiatric section of another hospital. I stood in the halls with my dad. This had been a forty-year-experience for him, but now his bank account was gone. What money he had earned and hoped to pass on to my brother and me was gone. He was fighting back tears.

I said, "Dad, what are we going to do?"

I'll never forget his words: "We'll make it somehow; we'll get along somehow." My dad was not a deeply religious man, but he was a believer and a great father. He had what I call *rockin' chair faith*—he was somewhat unshakable and staunch in his faith toward God. He didn't read his Bible much, and I don't think I ever heard him pray. He was pretty timid. He loved my mother very much. I'm sure you are wondering why I am telling you this.

The last few weeks of my mom's life were spent in a hospital bed not far from our home. My dad was there morning till night sitting in her room. When she died, I preached her funeral. It was hard, but I knew she was saved and loved the Lord, and now she was free from her torment. This was about the time in my life that I felt God calling me to deliverance and healing ministry. Many things were happening in my life and ministry.

A few weeks after her death my dad called me; his voice was shaking, and he was scared. I had never heard this in my dad's voice. I went to his house. He told me that after he went to bed, he saw my mother standing on the opposite side of the bed. He assured me that this was real and he was wide awake— he had just gotten into bed. He said that it was not flesh and blood, but it was her. He said, "I even spoke to her and told her to come on to bed."

He said, "Don, she sat down on the foot of the bed with her head turned slightly away from me. I slid my foot on that side of the bed to nudge her." His voice was trembling. "This spirit, or *thing*, slapped my foot away and turned toward me with the most frightening face I have ever seen." It was like a nightmare, but he was wide awake!

He wanted me to explain. He felt certain that no one would believe him, nor was there anyone he could talk with about it. Was it my mother? Of course not! Was the experience real? Yes. This is the kind of things that demons do. They cause deception and horrific terror. While this was a wide-awake vision, it was terror of the mind and very disturbing to my father.

I will never forget the fear in his voice. It may have been a demon that once lived in my mom; I don't know. I prayed and commanded any and all demon powers to leave him and the house in Jesus's name. He lived the remainder of his life without any torment of this kind. Why did I tell you this? Because this type of thing is far more common than you may believe. It is important for believers to discern and to try the spirits whether they are of God—this is outside the bounds of Scripture. It is clearly the deceptive work of demon powers.

Chapter 4

WHAT MAKES JESUS REJOICE?

W E KNOW FROM Scripture what makes angels rejoice; they rejoice when people accept Christ as Savior. Do you know what makes Jesus rejoice?

> In that hour Jesus rejoiced in spirit, and said, I thank thee, O Father, Lord of heaven and earth, that thou hast hid these things from the wise and prudent, and hast revealed them unto babes: even so, Father; for so it seemed good in thy sight. All things are delivered to me of my Father: and no man knoweth who the Son is, but the Father; and who the Father is, but the Son, and he to whom the Son will reveal him. And he turned him unto his disciples, and said privately, Blessed are the eyes which see the things that ye see.
>
> —LUKE 10:21–23

Look at the excitement in the above verses. The seventy disciples sent out by Jesus returned with joy from the results of their obedience. And Jesus rejoiced in the Spirit! This was like a team meeting after a great victory where the coach was praising his team for a good job. You might want to read this twice to get the full impact.

When you read Luke 10, you see that Jesus sent seventy men

to go in His name—thirty-five two-man teams. He appointed them to go before Him into every city and place that He would come. The parallel account in Matthew 10:1 reads: "He gave them power against unclean spirits, to cast them out, and to heal all manner of sickness and all manner of disease." He gave authority to His twelve disciples and then to seventy *rookies*—babes, if you will—to cast out demons and to heal all kinds of sickness.

Notice that when the thirty-five teams returned from their appointments, they returned with "joy," saying, "Lord, even the devils are subject unto us through thy name" (Luke 10:17). The Bible indicates they were exuberant. It was unrestrained joy. It was *all over their faces.* I wonder how they expressed that joy.

I vividly recall how I expressed it the first time I experienced it in Kingston, Ontario, Canada. I could take you right to the spot on the top step of the Kingston, Ontario, Federal Prison for Women. I had just ministered in my first deliverance meeting. I commanded demons to leave in the name of Jesus, and they obeyed. A tormented woman was set free.

I walked out of that prison, paused on the top step at the prison entrance, thrust the Bible in my right hand high above my head, and said, "Yes, in the name of Jesus, yes!" I left with joy. I'm pretty sure I know what these men felt when they returned to Jesus.

I know the joy of participating with the Holy Spirit and exercising the name of Jesus Christ against demons, sickness, and disease. But I wonder what Jesus was feeling when Scripture says Jesus rejoiced in the Spirit at their report.

In that hour Jesus rejoiced in the Spirit; Jesus is genuinely excited here also. Literally, the ancient Greek says He was thrilled with joy. God delights in using the weak and foolish things of this world to confound the wise (1 Cor. 1:27–29).

The ancient Greek word for *rejoiced* is referring to exceptional rejoicing and exultation. Do you think it might have been equivalent to an athlete's fist pump when experiencing victory? I think it was something like that—Jesus's joy makes Him break out into prayer. He praises God the Father for His wisdom, for His plan, and for His own unique relationship with God the Father—"I thank You, Father." How many times I have said, "Thank You...thank You...thank You," because of the joy of seeing people delivered.

Rejoice is really too weak of a word. It means, "exulted in spirit." The word *exulted* means, "to show triumphant joy." Jesus gave visible expression to His unusual emotions, while, at the same time, the words *in spirit* are meant to convey to the reader the depth of those emotions. This is one of those rare cases in which the veil is lifted from off the Redeemer's inner man. We, like the angels, desire to look into it with greater depth (1 Pet. 1:12).

As we look on this with reverential wonder, and as we perceive what it was that produced this ecstasy, we will also find rising in our hearts a measure of rejoicing in our spirit, an exaltation.

I think I see an unbridled smile and an expression of victory that could be seen as a fist pump or high five by Jesus. *Exulted*, remember, is to show or feel triumphant elation. The thirty-five two-team rookies had obeyed His Word, and the demons had obeyed their commands. Jesus is not only pleased; He is exulted. He feels triumphant joy, and He shows it.

I like the picture I see here. Jesus exulted and the Father exalted. It is my desire to bring exultation to Jesus and exaltation to the Father. One produces the other. This whole process, Jesus said, seemed good to the Father. If it makes Jesus rejoice and seems good to the Father, why are we not doing it in the church today?

Jesus made sure that the seventy men did not rejoice in the wrong thing. He basically said, "You have power over demons because I gave it to you; don't lose sight of why you have such authority." We are in Christ, and Christ is in us, and we are healed by the authority of His name. It's the response that must come.

You see, I am ever aware that the things I see and experience in this ministry have simply been revealed to me, that I qualify as not wise and prudent but as a babe in His sight. I wouldn't want it any other way. I believe today that Jesus rejoices when we act in His name and believe His Word. Maybe He gives a fist pump or a high five to the angels when Christians act upon faith in His Word. The angels do give high fives when people accept Christ; there is joy in heaven whenever one sinner repents.

Rejoice is too weak of a word. Jesus was exulted in spirit. Again, we, like the angels, may look into it briefly. Rejoicing in our victories leads to, "Thank You, Father," as it did with Jesus in Luke 10:21. Jesus said, "All things are delivered to me of my Father...and he to whom the Son will reveal them" (v. 22). God the Father gave it to Jesus, and Jesus gave it to us...to me, a babe in Christ.

Does it confound the wise? You be the judge. Authority as a believer is not received or understood through education and accomplishment. Really, it is not even discovered; it is revealed. It is not hidden; it just cannot be seen through carnal eyes.

Seeing Into the Darkness

Our spiritual perception is always affected by the amount of light that we have. The apostle Paul says that now we "see through a glass darkly." It is so important that as believers we walk in the light. There is power in darkness. Look at the truths revealed in one of the Bible's most familiar passages.

> And when he had sent the multitudes away, he went up into a mountain apart to pray: and when the evening was come, he was there alone. But the ship was now in the midst of the sea, tossed with waves: for the wind was contrary. And in the fourth watch of the night Jesus went unto them, walking on the sea. And when the disciples saw him walking on the sea, they were troubled, saying, It is a spirit; and they cried out for fear.
>
> But straightway Jesus spake unto them, saying, Be of good cheer; it is I; be not afraid. And Peter answered him and said, Lord, if it be thou, bid me come unto thee on the water. And he said, Come. And when Peter was come down out of the ship, he walked on the water, to go to Jesus. But when he saw the wind boisterous, he was afraid; and beginning to sink, he cried, saying, Lord, save me. And immediately Jesus stretched forth his hand, and caught him, and said unto him, O thou of little faith, wherefore didst thou doubt?
>
> And when they were come into the ship, the wind ceased. Then they that were in the ship came and worshipped him, saying, Of a truth thou art the Son of God.
>
> —MATTHEW 14:23–33

Peter made a good decision when he got out of the boat. He made a good decision when he got back in the boat. You never want to be out of the boat unless Jesus is out of the boat AND He has invited you to come with Him.

I wonder how many messages have been preached from this portion of Scripture. I wonder how many *doctrines* have been based upon this area of Scripture. Lack of faith and super faith are often the subject of different preachers at different times.

Jesus walking on the water may be the most well known of the miracles in the New Testament. Doesn't everyone know about it? The Sea of Galilee is about thirteen miles long and eight miles wide. The disciples were in the midst of sea. So Jesus walked at least four miles on the water to get to them. Some people suggest that this took place at the narrowest portion of the lake—what difference does that make? It was more than a hop, skip, and a jump. Weather conditions were not ideal. It was somewhere between three and six o'clock in the morning. Darkness and the wind were enough that the boat was tossed about on the waves. There were no lights in the midst of the sea; it was dark. Maybe it was a full moon, and there was no cloud cover, but the waves were boisterous—it was in the blackness of the night.

Not enough light lends to the possibility of deception. The disciples spotted Him—a figure coming toward them on the water. Obviously there was not enough light to see that it was Jesus. What would you have thought? Loch Ness Monster? They thought it was a spirit. (Interesting, they must have believed in spirits.) They were troubled and fearful. When Jesus sensed their fear and confusion, He said to them, "Be of good cheer; it is I; be not afraid" (v. 27).

With the wind whistling and the waves sloshing against the boat, Jesus must have been fairly close to them at that time; He spoke and they heard. He was close enough to have a conversation. He always is. It takes about an hour and a half to walk four miles on land; to my knowledge there is no evidence of how long it takes on water.

It is not necessary, nor, I believe, is it possible, to know how this was done. Did He condense the surface of the water? When God pleases, the depths are congealed in the heart of the sea: "With the blast of thy [God's] nostrils" He can control the sea (Exod. 15:8). Did He suspend the gravitation of His body, which was transfigured as He pleased? It is obvious that it proves His divine power.

God can as easily tread upon the waves of the sea, as recorded in Job 9:8, as He can ride upon the wings of the wind. He who made the waters of the sea a wall for the redeemed of the Lord makes them a walkway for the Redeemer Himself. He can appear with one foot on the sea and the other on dry land. Christ can choose whatever way He pleases to save His people.

He had sent His disciples ahead. He had told them He would catch up with them. I don't know if it ever crossed their minds that they had the boat. How would He meet up with them? Remember He had "constrained" them to do this. He insisted, virtually ordered them. They obeyed, and likely while He was praying and resting in a secret place, they found themselves in the midst of a stormy sea.

I would like to have listened in on the conversations on that boat. I have a feeling there was some discussion of how the ministry was being operated. I'm not sure, but probably some questions were being raised about why Jesus sent them into the storm. There may have been some unkind words about His leadership decisions. Oh, surely not; those things don't happen! They were probably encouraging each other and recounting how blessed they were to be a part of the group.

I wonder if the disciples ever criticized Jesus behind His back. I wonder if there was ever dissension about who got to be up front most, and if there was envy among the disciples. I'm just wondering. Regardless, Jesus appeared to the disciples, and He was walking on the water. He saw through the darkness of the night. He went into the darkness unafraid. He sees into our darkness as well and speaks, "Be not afraid." Seeing in the darkness removes the power of darkness.

He comes walking on top of the very obstacle that brings natural things down. He demonstrates His supernatural ability. He shows Himself to be Lord of all in this simple passage of Scripture—bigger than the elements, bigger than *nature's laws,* which, by the way, are principles of His that we simply discover. The sea dare not attempt to drown Him; He is the Creator. The winds whisper in His presence.

You think He can't come to you because of the magnitude of your problem? You think the water is too deep? The darkness that engulfs you is too great? The circumstances that hold you captive are too big for Him? You think He's scared? You think He doesn't know the situation? What? Darkness is an advantage for demon powers. They do their best work in darkness.

You think maybe He dozed off and was not aware of His promise to come to them? Psalm 121:3–4 reads, "He will not suffer thy foot to be moved: he that keepeth thee will not slumber. Behold, he that keepeth Israel shall neither slumber nor sleep."

He arrived at the boat right on time; the boat was going into the wind, and so was He. When Jesus was spotted and spoke to them, He spoke to their fear. He spoke cheer instead of fear! They were buzzing with excitement: "It's Jesus walking on the water! Look, it's Him!" Thomas may have said, "I doubt it." Others probably sensed the awe of it all and maybe said nothing. Peter, however, was so excited that he said, "Lord, if that is You, let me come out there with You." Jesus spoke only one word: "Come."

I believe He still invites us to come experience what He is capable of. In the boat was safety, but Peter crawled out with no life jacket into the *boisterous* sea. He walked a little bit on the water; his faith in Jesus's word was enough to experience what no other man has. This message is not about *getting out* of the boat; it is more about getting back in the boat.

If Jesus invites you out to come to Him, to experience a faith moment, by all means go. But when He gets in the boat, you get in the boat. Peace and safety are in the boat; fellowship with others is in the boat. Worship takes place in the boat. Some have ventured out of the boat and have had to be lifted back up by Jesus. The real key is in desiring to be where Jesus is!

Demons love to work in the darkness. When we can stay close to Jesus, His light banishes the darkness. Seeing into the darkness diminishes the demons' advantage. Darkness really is just the absence of light. Darkness has many characteristics that give advantage to demons. Where there is light, there is no darkness! Where we choose to position ourselves before God determines how and what we can receive from Him. Choosing to walk in light is a great big plus for believers! The first chapter of John tells us that Jesus is our life and our light.

> In him was life; and the life was the light of men. And the light shineth in darkness; and the darkness comprehended it not. There was a man sent from God, whose name was John. The same came for a witness, to bear witness of the Light, that all men through him might

believe. He was not that Light, but was sent to bear witness of that Light. That was the true Light, which lighteth every man that cometh into the world.

—JOHN 1:4–9

Walking in darkness is most often a choice.

Chapter 5

ARE ANGELS
PRINCIPALITIES AND POWERS?

A NGELS—PRINCIPALITIES AND POWERS? Of course they are. Most Christians automatically think about demons and dark powers when reference is made to principalities and powers. What about angels? Angels were here first!

A friend of mine told me that shortly after she arrived in the United States from Puerto Rico, she accepted Christ. She said, "I had not been here that long when I was driving my car and ran out of gas. I was alone, and even though I was near a gas station, I panicked a little bit because my car had stalled. It seemed from out of nowhere a young man walked up to me and offered to push my car. He pushed me right to the gas pump, and before I could get out of the car to thank him, he was gone." She said, "It must have been an angel. I still can't get over it; it had to be an angel."

I'm pretty sure you have heard a story like that; maybe you have even experienced something similar. Do angels do things like this? Yes, they do. Angels are apparently God's first creation. They have been around for a long time. This is exciting in itself. What is their interest in man? Are they all alike? Are angels aware of our needs? Do they come in response to prayer? What is their purpose? If there were no people on earth, would they be interested in the world? So many questions! Do they eat? What language do they speak?

I read an amazing story in a magazine about angels intervening in an unlikely plane crash. I was surprised to learn that one of the men in the plane crash, Eddie Weise, lived near where I live. I called Eddie recently, and he recounted the story to me.

Eddie said he never thought he would be a part of anything like this. He says, "I was just a passenger in the plane, just along for the ride." What a ride it was. Eddie still lives in Millsap, Texas. He and his wife help make up the population of less than four hundred people. Here is Eddie's spiritually stirring story.

> We were above the clouds, and the night was serene. As I marveled at the sensation of flying, I thought it must be just like the angels; they surely are all around us.
>
> I was with my friend David, who was piloting. We were in a Beechcraft Bonanza headed back to our local airport in Fort Worth. We had been in Oklahoma, where we'd taken our pastor and his wife. We'd had a prayer service before we left Texas, and people told us they'd linger at the church for a while to pray some more.
>
> There was talk of bad weather, so I was grateful for their prayers. Still, in my mind, there seemed no cause for alarm. Our flight was less than an hour, and I saw only calm on the horizon. The lights of Dallas were bright as we landed at Love Field to refuel.

Love Field was once the main airport in Dallas and is still very busy; it is located near the heart of the city. Eddie said they communicated with the tower and inquired about the weather. The tower reported that the weather was "A-OK," so they continued their journey. He said, "We were airborne only about ten minutes when thunder rumbled and lightning pierced the sky.

"Hold tight," David said. "Just twenty-five miles and we're home."

Eddie continued his story:

> We bounced around like a leaf in the buffeting wind. Our heads were thrown against the canopy of the plane. Then the view cleared, and we could see the airport ahead! David shouted. "There's more of this storm coming, but with any luck I'll make it in before it hits." I jerked back in my seat as he increased the speed. The plane lurched forward. We zoomed between two giant electrical towers, skimming above the transmission lines. The plane dipped to the left. *Wham!* It felt like the bottom dropped out. I gripped the arms of my seat. "Jesus!" I said in prayer. *Wham!* We were slammed, almost stopped in midair by something with enormous power.
>
> I was startled and cried out, "What was that? All at once we were flung backward. David pulled on the stick. We were falling! "Jesus!" I prayed again. This is it. When would the blackout come? I wondered. But it didn't. I was wide-eyed awake as the plane crashed into the ground, twisting, turning, its wheels digging into the dirt.
>
> We didn't move. Could we? The engine burst into flames. Lightning flashed all around us. I grabbed the door at my side. I couldn't open it. Frantic, I tugged at the handle. I pushed and shoved. It wouldn't budge.
>
> "I can't open the door!" I shouted. Then I felt a hand near mine. David! The door swept open. "Run!" David shouted. We leaped from the plane. The constant flashes

of lightning were almost as bright as day, and we quickly looked around. Our feet were deep in muddy grass. We'd crashed into a farm pasture, with no roads or houses nearby. Then I spotted a hangar in the distance. "There's the airport!" I shouted. We'd missed it by maybe half a mile.

We ran, afraid of an explosion. The plane engine burned, and the lightning hammered down with fierce, jagged force. David and I reached a fence a few yards away. "You OK?" David said. "I'm exhausted, but yeah," I said. We scrambled over the fence and then turned to look back. I stared with disbelief. The vision was clear in a blaze of fire and lightning. Two figures stood in front of the plane. Where had they come from so quickly, here in the middle of an open field? They were unlike any men I'd ever seen. These two towered above the aircraft, taller by three feet or more. Their skin glowed smooth like a baby's, and their shoulder-length hair shone like gold.

Eddie said he couldn't really describe what he saw.

Most amazing of all, somehow, through their clothes I could see the fire and lightning. Were my eyes playing tricks on me? "Let's get away from here," David said, as the skies burst and the rain poured down. *"Please, Lord, let it put out the fire in the engine."* We raced toward the safety of the hangar at the airport and both dropped to our knees. After a few moments we looked at each other. "I'll never know how you opened the door," I said. "We'd never have gotten out otherwise."

"I didn't touch the door," David said.

I was startled, somewhat stunned by his words. "But I saw your hand." David replied, "It wasn't mine." I could tell he'd understand what I was about to say. "Do you know what we saw?" I asked, overcome with wonder. David nodded, and I could see the wonder in his eyes too. When we compared the vision we'd witnessed, we came to the same conclusion. We had seen angels—two magnificent angels who had arrived to take charge and see to our safety.[1]

Eddie went on to tell me that several newspapers carried the story after it happened, one being the *Fort Worth Star-Telegram*. Though this happened several years ago, I remember reading about it. Pretty incredible! This amazing event happened not that many miles from where I live. I know you have heard and read many such accounts.

While there is no mention of angels in the following scriptural account, it is obvious that they were at work.

> And, behold, men brought in a bed a man which was taken with a palsy: and they sought means to bring him in, and to lay him before him. And when they could not find by what way they might bring him in because of the multitude, they went upon the housetop, and let him down through the tiling with his couch into the midst before Jesus. And when he saw their faith, he said unto him, Man, thy sins are forgiven thee.
>
> And the scribes and the Pharisees began to reason, saying, Who is this which speaketh blasphemies? Who can forgive sins, but God alone? But when Jesus perceived their thoughts, he answering said unto them, What reason ye in your hearts? Whether is easier, to say, Thy sins be forgiven thee; or to say, Rise up and walk? But that ye may know that the Son of man hath power upon earth to forgive sins, (he said unto the sick of the palsy,) I say unto thee, Arise, and take up thy couch, and go into thine house.

> And immediately he rose up before them, and took
> up that whereon he lay, and departed to his own house,
> glorifying God. And they were all amazed, and they glo-
> rified God, and were filled with fear, saying, We have
> seen strange things to day.
>
> —LUKE 5:18–26

He prayed, but the palsy stayed! Ever been there? You prayed, but the problem stayed? This man was hopelessly paralyzed. We don't know how old he was, nor do we know how long he had been in this condition. What I do know with some measure of certainty is that he had prayed, but he still had palsy and his hope was fading.

Hope, among its many definitions, is "holding on to the idea that something good may happen even if it is against great odds." It is not letting go of a dream or desire. This man's hope was surely fading. What a desperate place to be when it seems certain that your miserable situation is not going to change. Faded hope is when you feel very near to giving up and accepting an undesirable condition. As you read this account in Luke 5 or in Mark 2, you can see how he must have lived in *fading hope*.

Across town, in an undetermined location, was Jesus. Was He next door, in the next block? Jesus was in the house. Whatever the man's condition, help was closer than he could have imagined. It was not the Sabbath day, else Jesus would have been in the synagogue; this was just a "certain day," and the house was overflowing. All types of people—scribes, Pharisees, doctors, lawyers—helpers and hinderers, the helpless, the hearers, the heartless, and THE healer! They were all there. The Bible says they came to hear Him *and* to be healed of Him. Today we just come to hear Him. The Bible also says

the power of the Lord was present to heal them! Well, that makes a difference.

You would think the people would have been gracious and made a way for the man with palsy being carried on his bed; you would think they would have opened a passageway right to Jesus. The house was packed! Doorways and window openings were covered apparently by several rows of people. Demon powers often use God's people to prevent others from getting to Jesus.

I wonder what kind of faith these four men had. I wonder how they even convinced the palsied man to go with them. They had heard and seen something about Jesus; they knew something.

Clearly the Bible teaches us that faith comes by hearing the Word of God—in this case, the words of God. These four had heard enough to believe that Jesus would heal their friend, enough that the four carried him on his bed to get to Jesus. They likely had to persuade him to go.

Can you visualize the four men talking to him, each standing near one of the four corners of his blanket, ready to transport him? Can you hear the conversation? One guy saying, "Come on, man, I used to be blind and Jesus healed me."

The man may have reasoned, "Yeah, but this is my whole body. I'm a mess."

One of the other fellows may have said, "I once was deaf, but now I can hear."

"Oh, I know," he interrupts, "but I just don't know if I can believe for this."

The third guy may have said, "Come on with us, man; I used to be lame, and now I can walk."

"Mmm, I don't know…"

The fourth guy said, "Hey, my name is Lazarus; I used to be

dead!" I can see the man's faith release to the point that he is ready to go.

I don't know how far they carried the man, but it is not easy for four people to carry 150 to 200 pounds for any distance. Not only did they carry him a distance, but also they got up to the roof of the house with this man. They were determined, by faith, to get their friend to Jesus! They had once been in the grip of demons and darkness, disease and despair. They knew Jesus could do it. I'm sure they were strengthened and assisted by angels.

Let your mind create a good picture of this. Their faith saw beyond all kinds of obstacles. Their faith did not underestimate God. Jesus deals with the immediate and most outstanding need any man has. First the sin, then the sickness! Repentance and salvation must come before deliverance comes!

Matthew Henry says, "Sin is the procuring cause of all our pains and sicknesses.... The way to remove the effect, is, to take away the cause. Pardon of sin strikes at the root of all diseases, and either cures them, or alters their property."[2] What a great comment. The Bible says, "When Jesus saw their faith," He said unto him, "Man, your sins are forgiven." Jesus not only recognized the faith of others who believed for the man, but He also recognized that forgiveness of sin must precede healing. We see the same thing in deliverance and healing— first the sin, then the healing.

What peace must have come to this man's heart when the Son of God pronounced him clean, pardoned, and forgiven. That was his great need. I wonder how he may have felt, though, when the religious, "righteous" crowd began to question Jesus and His authority to forgive sins. He may have had a sinking, empty feeling. He was likely still suspended in the air by the grip of his four friends when the controversy arose.

Sadly the actions and words of that crowd today can rob the joy and peace of others. Why couldn't they just rejoice with his situation? Jesus, when He saw and heard all of this, said, "Whether is easier, to say Thy sins be forgiven thee; or to say, Rise up and walk? But that ye may know...Arise, and take up thy couch, and go into thine house" (Luke 5:23–24). All the man had to do was *obey*, and he did. This man walked back home glorifying God, probably doing some high stepping while the crowd was amazed and said, "We have seen strange things to day" (v. 26). Well, stranger things have happened!

A father came to Jesus on behalf of his sick daughter, who then died before they could get to her. Jesus went anyway to the house and spoke life into the twelve-year-old dead girl! Stranger things have happened.

A mother was in the funeral procession to bury her only son. She wept; Jesus saw her tears, stopped the procession, put His hand in the casket, and raised the man from the dead. He presented the son to the mother—stranger things have happened.

Two sisters wept and prayed for their sick brother. They wept after his burial; Jesus came and wept with them. He raised their brother out of the four-day burial in the grave. Stranger things have happened.

I heard that people got up out of their graves when Jesus got up out of His—stranger things have happened. Do you think your need is too great? It may be right around the corner; it may be just across town or perhaps through some friends who believe with you and for you. Stranger things have happened! You feel like you are in a hopeless condition and things will never get better? Stranger things have happened! A man waits thirty-eight years for an angel to stir the water. Jesus Himself stopped by!

Angels stir healing waters! Do angels come in response

to prayer by others? I believe they are absolutely in action regarding our faith and needs. I can *see* angels ministering all through the accounts of Jesus's meeting and ministering to people.

Are there baby angels? What is the gender of angels? Are they all spirit beings? I will try to answer these questions and many more. You will understand my interest in angels after reading the next chapter.

Chapter 6

"DAD, HAVE YOU
EVER SEEN AN ANGEL?"

PROBABLY THE QUESTION I receive most often is, "How did you get started in deliverance ministry?" Although there were some significant things that happened in my life that brought me to the area of deliverance, some that I have written about in previous books, my interest in demons was provoked by an experience with angels. I have been drawn to the supernatural not so much out of human curiosity as I have by God allowing me a few peeks into this spiritual realm. Everyone, it seems, wants to know about the spirit world, and it is super fascinating, but something piqued my interest several years ago, and I have been checking it out ever since. I was a seminary graduate and father of two young boys. I had a beautiful wife, and life was good.

My then seven-year-old son saw angels; they interacted with him, and I was present when it happened! What I am about to share caused me to seek more from God and from those who I believed had knowledge about the spirit realm.

While I cannot give you the sequence in which the *things* of God's universe were created, by believing God's Word, I do know that all things were created by and for Jesus. I know that angels existed before man, and they witnessed man's creation. They were created as super-intelligent beings, and much of God's will has been revealed to them. The entire Book of Revelation attests to this. I knew very little about the holy angels of God prior to this experience.

I want you to understand that what I am about to relate happened to a perfectly typical seven-year-old boy, my youngest son, Robby. Today, he is Dr. Rob and is a renowned neurosurgeon, but when this experience took place, he was in the second grade.

He had been saved about a year when this happened. He, like his older brother, trusted Jesus at an early age. They were not prompted. They came to Jesus, convicted by the Holy Spirit. The day before this happened, my wife had taken Robby to an allergy specialist. After being examined, the doctor advised that it would be helpful to have an air conditioning/heating system with special filters and equipment to minimize certain allergens.

Workers came the very next day to make bids on installing such a system. It was Wednesday, and our family went to church on that midweek day. However, workers were still there when I needed to leave for church. I excused myself, but before I left, Robby came to me and said, "Dad, can I go with you?" He had not eaten, and because of the circumstances, I told him to stay home with Mom and his older brother, Donnie. He said, "Wait, Dad, I'm going out in the backyard under that tree [a specific tree in our backyard] and read my Bible; where does it talk about my angels?"

I thought a moment and told him to read Matthew, chapter 18. "Take heed that ye despise not one of these little ones; for I say unto you, That in heaven their angels do always behold the face of my Father which is in heaven" (v. 10). He was only seven and could barely read, but he went out with his Bible as

I left. After church several people wanted to talk, some had problems, and others just made casual conversation. It was past Robby's bedtime when I finally got home, but he was up and waiting. He had made arrangements with his mother to sleep with me, because he "just wanted to talk."

Robby and I went to bed. The lights were out, and my wife and other son were asleep in another room. I asked Robby what he wanted to talk about. He said, "Dad, have you ever seen an angel?" I told him no, that I never had. He said, "I saw an angel, Dad, really, I saw two of them! While I was reading my Bible under the tree, I asked God if He would let me see *my angels*, and He did!" This caught me by surprise, and I began to cautiously question him. He sensed the doubt in my questions, and he began to cry. Through his tears he said, "I knew nobody else in the whole world would believe me, but I thought you would." Then he said, "Dad, they are here, they are in the room right now, and they look sad."

I saw nothing even though there was enough light to see the doors and windows. However, I did sense an awesome presence of God! I explained to Robby that I could not see them but assured him that I believed he did. I asked where they were, and he said that one was standing at the bedroom door and the other one standing right beside him. I was careful not to put words into his mouth but asked if they were small like little statues that he may have seen. "Oh, no, Dad, they are bigger than you; they're bigger than the door." I asked if they had long blond hair and looked like women, because I thought maybe he had seen paintings like this. "No, sir, one of them has dark hair, and one has blond hair, but it is short, and they're not girls; they're men."

I became increasingly more aware that God was letting him see what millions of Christians never get to see. Robby was not afraid, nor was he surprised. He told me, "I just knew God would let me see them 'cause He knows how much I love Him and how much I wanted to see my angels." I asked him if he could describe them to me, and without hesitation or forethought he said, "The one at the door is big and has short blond hair and looks kinda like Uncle Dick in Georgia. He has either two big wings or six little ones. I can't tell for sure, it's sort of foggy, but I believe he has three wings on each side. They sort of cover up his arms, and he has a black book in his right hand, nothing in his left hand." I asked if he had on a gown, and Robby said, "No, he has on really shiny white clothes, kinda like those soldiers wear in pictures. His belt is shiny white." I asked if he could see the angel's feet. He rose up in bed and said, "Yes, sir, he has on sandals laced up around his legs."

I asked about the angel standing at his side of the bed, and he giggled a little in excitement. "He looks kinda like me, Daddy, 'cept his hair is dark and he is a man." This is interesting. To me it is very interesting. The Jews believed in guardian angels; they even believed the guardian angel looked like the person over whom they watched. Recall when Peter was imprisoned, and the church was praying in Acts 12. The angel of the Lord released Peter, and he came to the house where prayer was being made (v. 15). They thought it was "his angel." I love these little confirmations.

He asked me if they would play with him, and I told him no, they were sent from God to watch over and protect him. I told him they only wanted him to worship God. "Every time you say Jesus or God, they look at you and smile," said Robby. I asked if he would describe them further. "Yes, he has either two big wings, or four little ones." He just couldn't be sure. He said it looked like little lines on their wings, but it wasn't really clear. "He has a sword in his right hand, and it goes straight up by his face, and a little red Bible, kinda like yours, or a book, in his left hand. His clothes are the same. They are really shiny white, Dad, really white."

He asked me if he could go with them. "Go with them?" I could barely hold back my tears; had God sent His angels for my son? I asked him why he wanted to go with them. He said, "'Cause they're so pretty, and I want to watch over you and Mom and Donnie so no one will ever hurt you." I explained to him that he could not be an angel because God has something better prepared for His children. He said, "They're smiling again, Dad."

Then he asked if he could talk to them. I really didn't know what to say because I had never seen an angel before, but I did know of many instances in the Bible where men and angels had conversations. I told him he could try. He turned to the one by his bedside and asked, so sweetly, "What's your name?" He said the angel replied either Judas or Jude. Robby seemed alarmed and asked if Judas wasn't a bad man. I explained to him that many other people were named Judas, or Jude, besides the one who betrayed Jesus. I knew my son would have never made up that name. This was very real.

He then asked the one at the door for his name and told me, even though he could barely hear, that he was sure the angel said it was Daniel. This experience lasted for about three hours. He asked me if he could touch them. Again I said, "Rob, I just don't know. If you want to try, I will go with you."

He said, "I think they will come to me if I ask." He asked in seven-year-old faith, "Daniel, will you come to my bed so I can touch you?" He was elated; immediately he said, "Dad, feel how soft their wings are." He took my hand and directed it, but I felt nothing, nothing but God's presence in a way I had never known before.

After a while he said, "I don't need to see you anymore tonight, but please stay and let me see you when I wake up." In a few minutes he was asleep, but not me. I could not sleep. I had been bathed in God's love and grace. I had experienced something that made me aware of God's presence as never before. I listened for God to speak to my heart. It was as though He was saying, "Go and tell the world about My holy angels."

I could not recollect hearing a message or preaching a message on God's supernatural beings. I am sure of this...if it had been me who had seen angels, I would not be speaking or writing about them. But now I can tell you this without any spiritual boasting or self-pride. It was not necessary to my faith to see them, but how my faith increased as I witnessed them working in my son's life. I can tell of their activity and ministry today with great assurance, even though I never have seen an angel.

The next morning, as I arose to leave for the day's work, I went to the bedside to kiss my sleeping son. I realized I was standing where one of *his angels* stood, or was standing. He opened his eyes and said, "I love you, Dad." He looked around the room and said, "Dad, they're still here." He smiled and closed his eyes in the sweetest experience I have ever known.

I chronicled everything. In the following weeks and months I read more about angels than ever before. I interviewed numerous people and checked every detail my son related with God's Word. There was no conflict but rather abounding evidence. He has told me, and only me (he would not talk about the angels to anyone else), of a few occasions where they had appeared to him since that night. Once as he was taking a test at school, he said he was getting confused and was about to cry. He said, "I knew the answer, but my mind wouldn't think." Just before tears came, his angel Daniel appeared and said simply, "Now think, Robby," then the angel disappeared. "Dad, he didn't tell me any answers, but my mind got smart again."

He told me that once, as he ran outside to recess, there were two groups of kids playing. As he started toward one, Daniel appeared in front of him and said, "Don't go over there, Robby. You will get hurt." He said he has seen them a few times when his mother drove him home from school.

"Daniel always stands outside of Mom's car door, and Judas by mine. They don't fly; they just go beside the car." On another occasion he told me of being in our backyard playing. "Mom called me once to come in, but I didn't go," he said. "Daniel came and stood in front of me and said, 'Go on in now, Robby.'" He would often see them on the school playground, standing beside a tree watching him. Now I know there will be some who read this who will not believe it. My purpose for sharing this is not for you to believe it, but to believe God! Believe Him, believe His Word, and believe that His angels are ministering spirits sent forth to minister for them who are heirs of salvation.

Once he told me with excitement, "Dad, angels can move cars just like this." He extended his arm as if he was pushing something out of the way. He then told me of a time when he was in the car with his mom, and a car tried to change lanes for an exit on the freeway, almost hitting them. At another time our family was returning home from a visit at my parents' house. It was on a residential street and after dark. He leaned over from the backseat and said, "Dad, they're here." I had told him to tell me anytime they appeared to him. "They are on the outside of the car, one on each side." I asked if they were flying, he said, "No, Dad, they just move as the car moves." He sometimes seemed frustrated that I couldn't see what he saw.

I could tell you more from this experience, but I won't; for now I just want you to know what sparked my interest in the spirit realm. God began to reveal to me that there is so much more! I will give you scriptural reasons why I believe this and give some accounts of how God opened my eyes of faith.

I recorded the account of my son's experience; I put it in an envelope, sealed it, and dated it. He was seven years old; I mentioned this earlier. I wrote his age on the envelope in years, months, and days. He was seven years, seven months, and seven days old. This means absolutely nothing to most people, and understandably so. Those who study Scripture closely, however, know that God's *perfect number* or God's number of completion is the number seven. Now as I wrote his age and the three sevens appeared, I became curious as to how many days he had lived. To my amazement the figure was 2,777 days. That may not be of interest to you, but it was to me.

He asked me one day if it was OK to tell God he was satisfied and didn't need to see them anymore. I suppose it was beginning to overwhelm him. I told him to thank God, and he did. One day after he had stopped seeing his angels, he asked me a curious question: "Dad, do angels eat?" I asked him to go get his Bible and read Psalm 78:25, which says, "Man did eat angels' food: he sent them meat to the full." He came back to me and said, "It looks like they eat meat."

As we drove home from church one day, my older son said, "Dad, I don't want you to think I didn't listen to the sermon, but guess how many songs in our song book talk about angels?" I thought back over the service and remembered a line from one of the songs: "Where bright angel feet have trod."[1] I knew this must have stimulated his interest. He said, "Of the first one hundred songs, seventeen of them have the word *angel* somewhere in the song."

Stir your mind to think of God's holy angels and their presence. Scripture says in Matthew 18:10, "Take heed that ye despise not one of these little ones; for I say unto you, That in heaven their angels do always behold the face of my Father which is in heaven." Wow! I'll address this more later. Their angels—plural—always behold the face of God!

Chapter 7

HEAVENLY VISITOR TO MY WIFE

I WAS PLAYING GOLF recently with my pastor and the founder and owner of the second largest Christian television network in the world. I was there as his guest. Between holes he asked me if I was about to get over my wife's death. "No," I said. "I don't know if I'll ever get over it, but I am getting through it." Marcus Lamb, of Daystar Television, had called me the day after my wife's death and prayed with me. He offered very consoling words and genuine kindness. I was very grateful for that; I was also glad to be his guest on the golf course this day, more than a year after Peggy's death.

One of the most difficult things for me to do since her death is to talk about it. It is hard to write about it. We were both under twenty when we got married; she's all I had ever known. I will tell you some of the details surrounding her untimely death to encourage you. If you haven't experienced something like this, you most certainly will. Loss is horrible; I don't know a better word for it.

Probably most husbands would say what I'm about to say out of respect, but I say it because I genuinely believe it. I had the best wife ever. She took care of me, she supported me, she was proud of me, and I knew it. Wow, that's so important. I don't think I could describe how she *spoiled* me. I don't think

I took it for granted, but I had learned to depend on her. She took care of *stuff* and let me minister. I joked with her constantly, she liked it, and I liked doing it. I played pranks on her almost every day.

Sometimes I would lie awake at night planning the next trick, just to hear her laugh or exclaim, "Don!" She laughed, she smiled, and she made everyone feel better just by her presence. She was so innocent and pure. She was a lady in every sense of the word. She was the most anointed piano player I have ever heard. When she played, there was peace. She would play sometimes at our ministry nights, and the presence of God would bless so many people.

She was from Georgia. Her dad worked for the FAA, and they moved several times to relocate for his job. I met her when she was a senior at Haltom High School in Fort Worth. A mutual friend had arranged a blind date—that was it. A few weeks later she accepted Christ in the front seat of my car on a church parking lot.

Fifty-two years had passed. She worked out three times a week; she walked every day and was extremely observant to nutritional guidelines. I guess you could say she was a picture of health, always smiling, always positive and energetic. Then I took her one day to see a cardiologist, and she never came back home.

A few years prior I had to have surgery on my spine in the neck area. It was necessary to be cleared by a cardiologist before they could do surgery. I had an imaging test that uses X-rays to view the blood vessels in your body. This is called an angiogram. I was cleared and had a successful surgery. The cardiologist did, however, suggest I have periodic checkups. Generally Peggy would go with me to the doctor's office in Plano, Texas. One day while she was with me, she told the doctor that she would like to get an angiogram done. After a preliminary visit and some tests, the doctor agreed to do the angiogram. Peggy knew something. The doctor didn't, I didn't, no one else did, but she did.

On Wednesday, November 10, I took her to the hospital for the test. Now, since I had had a similar test a year or so prior, I knew it was fairly simple and believed we would be back home in a few hours. After getting her back to the test area, I went outside to the waiting room to find that there were friends there, two of my best friends. I could not understand why they were there, but I appreciated them coming. Two ladies were there from my wife's Bible study group, one being her best friend, Cathy Thayer.

Peggy knew something, something I didn't know until after her death. She had told her friend Cathy that she had been having chest pains at night, and on more than one occasion she had seen Jesus by her bedside, and she was not afraid! She told of such warmth in His presence. She said, "He extended His arms toward me. I felt such love in His presence." But she had not told me; she didn't want me to be concerned.

My friends were at the hospital because Peggy had called them and asked them to come to be with me. I had no idea. After the test the cardiologist came out and came straight to me; she showed me images of her heart. She said, "I can't fix this with stints." The blockages were in places that stints could not go. "She needs triple bypass surgery in the next four to forty-eight hours." I still did not know what she had told to our friend Cathy. I don't think I can describe the feelings; my mind was racing and entertained all of the possibilities...but I never questioned God, and we began the next step.

I went back to talk with Peggy; she had tears in her eyes. I know now that her great concern was for me and our family.

She had already seen and experienced heaven's presence. The cardiologist was not a surgeon. A heart surgeon came to see her before it was decided where the surgery would take place. I wanted to ride with her, as she would be transported by ambulance to the best heart hospital in the area. I was not allowed to go, so I drove back some forty miles to Bedford to get things she needed for the hospital. What a long emotion-filled drive. I prayed, but I didn't know how to pray except to trust.

I got back to Plano and the massive hospital complex. There was construction at the hospital for new additions to the already large facility. I hurried to her room. I went to the wrong building but eventually got to where she was. This was on Wednesday. Her funeral was the following Monday.

The triple bypass surgery was the next day. As the news began to spread, friends came from all over to visit and to pray. After the surgery everything seemed to go well; she was awake, and all of the reports were good. Friday, as she was doing breathing exercises, something happened. There was a ruptured mitral valve, and after hours and hours of trying to determine what was wrong, the doctor decided on another surgery to replace her mitral valve. It was after midnight and early in the morning hours of Saturday.

Saturday evening our pastor came to see her. He brought his twelve-year-old daughter, who loved Peggy so much. Peggy loved her. Gabrielle had to stay in the surgical waiting room down a long hallway and around a couple of corners. Many people were there. I don't *know* this, but I had a sense that Peggy had already died; she was now on a ventilator. I won't say there was a peace that came over me because it was like nothing I've ever experienced, but there was a *knowing*. Many times during that five-day period I had asked the Lord to just give me some assurance that she would be OK. The assurance never came, but strength did.

My pastor, Dr. Frank Harber, told me that on the way home that night his daughter said, "I saw Ms. Peggy."

"How could you see her?" he asked. "It was impossible for you."

"I saw her," Gabrielle said. She described the room Peggy was in with every detail; she described how she looked. "I asked God to let me see her, and He did." Actually Gabrielle had prayed that God would make it possible for her to physically go back to the room. He let her see Peggy, though she never left the waiting room. I don't know exactly how angels do this kind of work, but I am confident of it. I have since asked Gabrielle about that experience, and she beams with a big smile and says, "God let me see her!"

Her funeral was a celebration. How she loved the song "I Can Only Imagine." I am finding it very hard to write about this. The chapel was overflowing; the Spirit of God was so obvious in His presence. Earlier that day Cathy had told me of Peggy's experience—that she had been seeing Jesus and was not afraid, and of the special description of the warmth of His presence. I was not surprised, but I immediately wondered why she did not tell me—but I knew she would know that I would know and was again looking out for me. My oldest son was going through her Bible and found this note to me.

I will paraphrase it here.

> Don, I think I'm going to be all right, but I want you to know that I have been seeing Jesus at night; He has come to my bedside. I know it's Him. I'm not scared. I'll be all right, and you'll be all right.
> Here are our bank account numbers...

Here are the ministries we are supporting, and I want
to continue to support them.

Just know I am OK, and you'll be OK.

Love,

Peggy

Wow! Was it really Jesus who appeared to her? I believe it
was. Could it have been an angel from His presence? I don't
know. I prefer to think it was Jesus.

Hebrews 12 tells us we are surrounded by a great cloud of
witnesses. These are the people of faith mentioned in chapter
11: Noah, Abraham, Isaac, Jacob, Joseph, Moses, Gideon, Barak,
Samson, Jephthah, David, and Samuel and the prophets and
believers from all ages, and now, Peggy!

While I was ministering at a church in Houston, a man I
do not know came and wanted to talk with me after church.
I will mention more about this in the next chapter. Now,
talking to me after church is not easy to do, because people
in our ministry *protect* me. I have never requested this, nor
would I, but because they love me, they often rush me out
of meetings and to a place of respite. This man insisted he
needed to talk with me; he said he had a special word from
God for me.

One of our ministry team workers took me to him. The
man introduced himself and said he had had a vision of
heaven, actually that he had been there as an observer. He
told me that like the apostle Paul, he also had seen and heard
things that he could not describe. But he said, "I also saw
people whom I knew on this earth who had died and gone
to heaven." After a bit more of his story he said, "The Holy
Spirit wants me to tell you that Peggy is very aware of you
and her family, and that she often bends the ear of God on
your behalf."

This man didn't know me; he only knew Peggy's name by reading about her death. I still don't know who he was. I found his words comforting, especially in light of what you will read next.

Chapter 8

BONES AND BONUSES

I GUESS YOU COULD say that what I am about to share was beyond my expectations. Actually I don't know if I had expectations other than in knowing God loves me a lot more than I am able to comprehend. It's difficult to know where to start with this story. But I want to share it with you for encouragement. As you just read, in 2010 my wife died unexpectedly. She was, in everyone's mind, a picture of health. It has been the most difficult thing I have ever had to deal with; really, it has been indescribable pain, and yet God's grace has been very rich, and I have found comfort from His Holy Spirit, His ministering angels, and great friends.

I am not writing to complain, for I am blessed. About six months after her death I experienced a ruptured appendix and emergency surgery. I was in the hospital for ten days. I actually hold the record for the largest ruptured appendix at the Hurst-Euless-Bedford hospital. Those things happen; everyone can tell a story about unexpected events in life. My biggest concern was for someone to take care of my bulldog, Dolly, who had been my faithful companion for eleven years. She was well cared for, so why am I telling you this?

I knew the time would come when my dog would die, and inwardly this was very heavy on my heart. I didn't talk to anyone about it, but it was there. Less than six weeks after the surgery, I had a three-day seminar in Houston that would include five services. The church was a Nigerian church. There were people at the seminar who had come from various parts of the country, some from various parts of the world. One family of nine had traveled from California and was staying in the church parking lot in a travel trailer. I did not know this until the close of the final service on Sunday evening.

Sometimes God singles you out for a blessing. Many of our team members were with me for this seminar. I'm glad, because they were firsthand witnesses of this miracle as well. They are all witnesses.

At the close of the last service the pastor asked if I would go into the church lobby and sign books for people. I was glad to do this. The first lady who came up to me was from the family of nine from California. She was the mother of seven children. I found out they were originally from Montana but had driven from a meeting at Bethel Church in Redding, California, to attend our seminar. Her name is Dari. With a big smile on her face she handed me a scroll with a ribbon around it. I was puzzled at first. "Open it," she said. I opened it, and there was a picture of a bulldog puppy and this letter:

> Dear Don,
>
>   We cannot fully express into words how your ministry has changed our lives. God has used you to be a doer of the Word and show people how to receive their freedom. God spoke to my wife in a vision last night about purchasing a bulldog for you. She will be healing to your heart and will bring joy and comfort to you. She asked for the Lord's angels to minister for you, for your grief to be lifted, and for healing of a broken heart.... Eleanor (the puppy) is from truly exceptional

world-class European English Bulldog bloodlines.... We have made arrangements for her to be driven to an address of your choice.

With love,

John, Dari, and kids

Pictures of a thoroughbred English bulldog named Eleanor (Ellie) were included in the scroll—a two-thousand-dollar bulldog puppy bred near Kansas City, purchased via the Internet. I was overwhelmed. ONLY God knew my heart, surely not this lady visitor. Tears filled my eyes, but I still didn't know how special this was. I could imagine trying to explain this in response to a normal question like, "Where did you get your bulldog?" "Well, let's see. I was preaching at a Nigerian church in Houston, a lady from California purchased a bulldog for me via the Internet from a breeder in Kansas City, and she was delivered to me at a mobile home park in Denton." What?

They gave me a phone number and e-mail address so I could contact them when I was ready for the delivery. The next morning our ministry team went back to the Dallas-Fort Worth area. I didn't know where they went. I still didn't know they were a family of nine living in a travel trailer.

As I thought about it, I thanked God, and in a couple of days I called them. They didn't know where I lived, and I didn't know where they were. I talked with the husband, John. He told me they thought I lived in the Dallas-Fort Worth area, so they had rented a space at a mobile home park in North Texas until the transaction took place. He told me that Eleanor was being driven to them, and they would transfer her to me on Monday; this was a week later.

Monday? Hmm, I already had an appointment for Monday evening. I looked up the address of the mobile home park and found it was less than a mile from where I had the already scheduled appointment! Amazing! I had never been to this town some forty-five miles from my home. Eleanor was to be delivered to them about five thirty; I had an appointment there at seven o'clock... wow! I finished my meeting and literally drove right around the corner to pick up "Ellie." Team members Fred and Nesta Partin drove me there; they were familiar with the location. They had also been at the meeting with me in Houston.

This was becoming like a chapter right out of the Bible, and it was about me. God and I knew, even if no one else did! They presented me with the puppy, and we talked; eventually I asked, "Where will you go from here?"

John said, "That all depends on you; right now you are our assignment!" This statement still intrigues me: "Right now you are our assignment."

He said they would like to stay a few days, and his entire family would like to come for one-on-one deliverance ministry. They felt God was calling them to be able to minister to others. The family stayed, and all went through deliverance the following week. After the sessions, prior to them leaving, Dari said to me, "Don, God gave me another vision for you, but I don't want to upset you." I encouraged her to share it. She first explained to me how she had experienced so much grief in her life and how she could see the pain of loss in my life.

Then she said, "In this vision I was out of my body and in my spirit; I was on the edge of heaven. There was a veil separating me from those on the inside. I saw a group of people talking, and one of the ladies in the group turned and walked toward me. She was beautiful and had the biggest, brightest smile. She came up to me and only said with a huge smile, "Tell Don I'm OK!"

I knew! Tears filled my eyes. I knew! Dari had never met my wife, but she described her perfectly.

The family left and are now back in the Northwest part of the country. It was like a chapter out of the Bible and I was featured. I cannot adequately describe how special this has been for me. My faithful bulldog, Dolly, died the day after Christmas; what a sad day. My new friend Ellie brings me comfort and joy. I hope this encourages you. God is so aware of your heart and desires. He's bigger than you think He is and wants so much to just love us! Was this the work of angels? Without doubt! I'm not sure how it all fits together here. I'm sure that the Holy Spirit, who is God, gives direction to angels and doubtlessly works in conjunction with them. It is interesting that the angels minister *for* us and the Holy Spirit ministers *to* us. I love being a participant!

Chapter 9

AN ANGEL VISITS
MY GREAT-GRANDFATHER

OFTEN GOD BRINGS to my remembrance events in my life that involved angelic activity. I must have been four years old when this happened, but I remember the experience. My family lived in the north Texas city of Sherman. We often rode on what was called an *interurban* from Sherman to Denison, only ten miles away, to visit my grandparents. This was the Texas Electric Railway System, linking Denison and Dallas. Not only did it bring the mail, salesmen and new products to small towns and their stores, but it also gave rural residents a means to get to "Big D" somewhat cheaply and safely.

It seems I can almost hear the *clickety-clack* and feel the sway of the railcars. I remember the tracks that were embedded on the main streets of the cities of Denison, Sherman, and McKinney. Some of the tracks remain today. There is a museum dedicated to this form of travel in Plano, Texas, near Dallas.

I can't tell you much of anything that happened when I was this age, but this memory lingers. One day our family rode to Dallas to see my mother's grandfather who was dying. They lived on Grand Avenue in the Fair Park section of Dallas. What I recall most is the discussions between family members, my mom's aunts and uncles. You see, my great-grandfather was dying, and he had told the family that he was visited by an angel the day prior, and the angel told him to gather his loved ones together and the angel would come back for him at 3:00 p.m. the next day. This was the next day!

At 3:00 p.m. my great-grandfather died. I remember the house and the room where he died. There was a calm, reverent excitement. It was like a *holy buzz* in the house. My mother's aunts and uncles, whom I did not know, were talking, though through tears, about the goodness of God. I'm not sure how I remember that day, yet when I think about it now, I wonder how I could not remember it. I guess that was my first experience and first memory about angels.

I am spiritually stirred at the working of angels in our lives. I am also curious about man's reluctance to talk about it. Testimonies are consistent. No new revelations. God's Word is complete! Appearances follow the biblical pattern. Angels appear. They speak. They disappear. They reappear. There is a heavenly touch in each experience that cannot be adequately shared with others; some of the experiences are for the individual only. Some come as an assurance. Some come as a warning. Some come to bring your attention to a segment of God's Word. Some come and minister without our knowledge, unaware.

God created angels to serve Him and to serve His people. If there is a constant theme in the Bible, it is Jesus! If there is a consistent truth, it is the existence and ministry of angels— they are real. The angels break into time, they do their job, they leave—or at least in their visibility to man. One of the things we know for sure about angels is that they are spirit beings; they are invisible but can on occasion reveal themselves to man.

Angels bring you closer to Jesus. They seek to magnify Him. They protect. They come as directed by God, often in answer to prayer. They appear in a form always recognized as being from God. They never leave the believer confused. They are all around us. Angels are not the chubby little babies that shoot cupid arrows. They are not feminine; they are always referred to as masculine. The Bible does not say that angels sing, but it is certainly a common belief that they do. If they do, it must be like something we have never heard.

I remember the period in my life when I felt God was calling me to ministry. I was nineteen years old; I still shared a bedroom with my younger brother in our home in Haltom City, Texas. In the summer we always slept with the windows open. This was before our family could afford air-conditioning. One night I heard the most beautiful music. I strained to hear it more clearly because it was faint. The music was distant, yet it was real; it was almost too good to be music. As I listened, there was a peace that came over me; it seemed like it penetrated to the core of my being. Was it the presence of angels? Was it God's Holy Spirit? Did God just crack the door of heaven to let me hear? I really don't know except I know it was real, and I know I have never heard music like that before or since.

I'm pretty sure if we could lift back the veil from heaven that we would hear music. I know that when angels come to us from God's presence, they bring some of that presence with them.

For a couple of years I ministered to little children as an associate pastor. I have talked with children from all walks of life. I have seen little black children come to know Jesus. I have seen a host of little white children come to know the Savior. I have talked with little brown children, and they too received Jesus. The little children mirror a little bit of heaven when I see them.

I have asked many of them if they would like to see an angel. All said yes, but this is what is amazing; some told me that they had already seen angels. Somehow, through God's amazing grace, little children are more ready to believe, more ready to see all that God wants for them. I thank God for little children! It is sometimes a sad transition when little children grow into the big children and have their faith tarnished by life. They are then not so quick to believe. As I write, study, and pray about God's message concerning angels, I become increasingly more aware of *their presence.*

One of my all-time favorite deacons in the Dallas-Fort Worth area told of angels ministering in his Christian life. He told me of a preacher who refused to die when his stomach was eaten with cancer—literally eaten to the point of the skin being laid open. He said the dying saint simply told those around him that God's angels had told him he would not die. The doctors said he had no chance. The nurses could not even go into the room because it was so horrible looking. Miraculously the stomach wound was healed. The cancer disappeared. The man lived and walked away from that hospital. God's angels cannot fail, because God cannot fail. With tear-filled eyes he shared this experience and said, "I wish more people would tell of God working in their lives." I do too! His holy angels are busy today!

In the discussion I mentioned a newspaper account of a little five-year-old girl in Foyil, Oklahoma. The little girl was asleep at one end of their mobile home; her parents were asleep in the opposite end. A fire broke out in the center of the mobile home, and the flames separated her from her sleeping parents. One of the men told me he knew the family personally.

He told in detail of what really happened. She said her angel awakened her and told her to go and tell her parents that their home was on fire. The child told of how the beautiful white angel held back the flames so she could get through the small passageway.

Further, the deacon said, "Reporters tried to confuse her by cross-examining her with questions for hours, but her story did not change." She knew what had happened. He also mentioned that this has had a tremendous impact upon the spiritual lives of that family, their loved ones, and friends. The reporters were convinced *enough* for the story to make the major wire services. God's supernatural work is worthy of reporting! However, His holy angels do not have to make the headlines to cause me to see them at work!

I recognize their activity and thank God for it.

God's Measuring Stick for Truth

For the word of God is quick, and powerful, and sharper than any twoedged sword, piercing even to the dividing asunder of soul and spirit, and of the joints and marrow, and is a discerner of the thoughts and intents of the heart.

—HEBREWS 4:12

It is important in today's Christian walk that we be discerning disciples—not only followers of truth but also discerners of truth. Someone once asked me, "Do you have the gift of discernment?" Yes, I do; I have the King James Version. The Word of God is a discerner.

Seems everyone wants to hear from God; everybody wants "a word." If you want to hear from God, you must hear His Word. God has spoken through His Word, and His Word is the discerner of the *thoughts* and intents of the heart. Simply, your thoughts, your *thoughts from God*, must line up with the already written Word of God. We must come into agreement with the Word of God. It is interesting, in the above verse, that the Word of God is able to invade our entire being—spirit, soul, and body. An absolute key for genuine freedom is spiritual alignment; that is, our spirit agreeing with what God says in His Word; our soul—mind, will, emotions, and personality—believing and speaking what God's Word says; and our flesh agreeing in obedience to the truth of God's Word.

There is an interesting verse of Scripture written by James to believers: "Do ye think that the scripture saith in vain, The spirit that dwelleth in us lusteth to envy?" (James 4:5). What? The spirit that dwells in us? But if I'm a believer, only the Holy Spirit can dwell in me; is that what you are thinking? What spirit do you suppose James is referring to here? Most likely our human spirit, but maybe evil spirits that can find a place in our soul and body. Evil spirits must be cast out; our human spirit must be cast down. There must be agreement in our being for there to be healing and fullness of God's presence.

You see, the Word gets into even the "joint and marrow," and the Word brings healing. Coming into agreement with truth that God has already spoken allows us to receive and apply the promises of the Word.

Whenever God speaks, whatever He says automatically becomes law. In His legal system alignment with truth brings freedom. Now the opposite is true as well. Rebellion, or refusal to receive His Word as truth, means we believe a lie, and the lie empowers demons. Empowered demons bring destruction, death, disease, and further deception to the believer. The job of every demon is to steal, kill, and destroy. The problem is that believers don't believe—more accurately, our belief is often tempered with conditions.

The Word of God is alive! It is alive and powerful. How can that be? "In the beginning was the Word, and the Word was with God, and the Word was God.... All things were made by him; and without him was not anything made that was made.... And the Word was made flesh, and dwelt among us" (John 1:1, 3, 14).

The Word of God is *alive* because Jesus is the Word. It is powerful because Jesus is the Word! What an incredible truth! When you speak the Word, you actually speak His presence right into your life and your situation. "Thy word is truth" (John 17:17). Discerning disciples must weigh *words* against God's Word. It is truth that liberates, and His Word is *truth*.

When Mary was holding the baby Jesus in her arms, I wonder if she knew that she was holding the one who was holding all creation in His grip. Maybe she did, but I doubt that she could possibly comprehend that He was in the beginning with God, and that He was and is God. Could she have known that He spoke everything into being and that when He speaks, all of creation obeys?

I think also that we are not able to receive the magnitude of power and authority that is ours in His name. I believe it is a little more than simply speaking His name; it is believing that His name is above every name. It is living daily, moment by moment in that amazing truth. His Word is truth. We are empowered by the truth of His Word, the presence of His Holy Spirit, and by exercising His name in our lives!

So people say that *truth* sets you free. Actually, it is more than that; it is *knowing the truth*. Perhaps it is even more than that—knowing and acting upon truth sets you free.

Chapter 10

RECOGNIZING THEIR
WORK IN OUR LIVES

WHILE WORKING FOR the local electric company, going to seminary, and directing a prison ministry, I also preached revivals and "filled pulpits" for other preachers. I had been invited to preach a revival meeting at the St. Paul Reformed Baptist Church where Rev. Frank Howard, now deceased, was pastor. I had been praying for one of my fellow office workers who, by his own admission, was not saved. I always invited him to wherever I might be preaching. I did not expect him to come, but I asked him anyway. Certain circumstances in his life had driven him to a turning point.

Tuesday night when I arrived at this church, an African American church in the Stop-Six area of Fort Worth, my friend was already there. He was searching; all he needed was Jesus. I preached about Jesus, for there is no other message. The time came for me to extend an invitation. As God's people sang and prayed, I could sense the struggle in his life. I felt certain he was ready to accept Christ, but something happened. The phone in the pastor's office rang, again and again—you could hear it, and it was somewhat disruptive. The pastor's wife went to the office to answer. My heart sank; it seemed the Spirit was quenched. In my mind I blamed Satan. My friend was not saved; no one was. The phone ruined everything.

Before the benediction was given, the pastor's wife announced that a lady had called and requested prayer. She said the woman's name was June Ramsey* (now deceased), and she felt extremely depressed. She said she just looked in the phone book to call a Baptist church. The pastor's wife smiled and said the lady didn't realize she was calling a black church and was surprised when she told her they had a *white* evangelist. But she did request our prayers.

After church I asked if she had gotten the address. "No, I just didn't think to do that," said the pastor's wife. I intended to visit the woman the next day. I felt certain I could get her address at work. The next morning my lost friend even helped me look for the address. Our efforts failed. We tried the city directory and a crisscross reference telephone book, but we could not find her address. My friend said, "I don't guess God intended for you to visit her."

"I guess not," I said. "I sure don't know where she lives." I went to my desk where my secretary had placed the names and addresses of customers to be contacted for the day. On the top of the contact sheets was a request for a voltage check and possible low delivery voltage. The customer's name—June Ramsey, and of course, her address was there also. I took the work order and placed it in front of my unsaved friend. He said, "I don't believe it...I don't believe it!"

What he meant was he couldn't help but believe it. I went to the home of June Ramsey. I checked to make certain that the proper electrical voltage was being delivered to her home. I assured her that it was and prepared to leave. I felt I had to say something, but the opportunity had not yet arisen. The

---

* Not her real name

elderly saint of God said, "I had the strangest thing happen last evening." She continued to tell of how she felt so low and depressed that she just had to have prayer by God's people. She told me she was intrigued by the name of a church as she looked through the phone book. "It seemed to stand out!" she said. "It was the Greater St. Paul Reformed Baptist Church, and to top it off, it was a black church and they were in revival with a white evangelist."

"Would you remember the evangelist's name if you heard it?" I asked. I told her my name again. She looked at me silently for a moment, and then tears began to well up in her eyes. Then she burst forth with praise for God's goodness. She did a little "holy dance"—she was amazed. So was I. We had prayer, and I left.

That evening at church my friend was there again when I arrived. I preached about Jesus. The invitation came, and so did my lost friend! Praise God! He poured out his heart, let Jesus come into his life, and was gloriously saved. Did the angels play a part in this experience? Did they visit June Ramsey? Why did she call my office the day before? Why was my lost friend exposed to all of God's mysterious workings? Yes, I believe God set His holy angels in action. "There is joy in the presence of the angels of God over one sinner that repenteth" (Luke 15:10). When my friend let Jesus into his life, I knew the angels were rejoicing!

One day I sat in the study of one of the most respected preachers in the state of Texas, a man who was pastor at one of the landmark churches in the city of Fort Worth. He has entertained foreign diplomats at the request of our presidents; he has preached at the nation's largest conventions. I talked with him about angels. I did not tell him about my son's experience; we just talked and the subject of angels came up. He said, "Not everyone believes that angels still minister today, but I certainly do." He then told of an experience he had while in high school. His father was pastor of a church, and he had four brothers who also were preachers. He said, "In my mind I was determined just to be a regular fellow—get a job and a family."

He described the parsonage where he lived in Austin, Texas. He mentioned outside stairs that led to his room on the second floor. He told me that when his high school girlfriend would come to see him, she would always *jump* onto the steps with a familiar jump, and he could hear her coming. He also mentioned that she died prematurely just prior to the event he was about to relate.

He told me he had arrived home from a very tiring football practice. "I took a hot shower and was relaxing on my bed when I heard that same *jump* on the staircase that I had heard so many times before. I got up and looked, but of course I knew it could not be her."

He said he went back to the bed, and in an instant she appeared in the form of an angel. "She was there just for a fleeting moment, then she was gone." He told me he did not understand it all, but something from that *angelic appearance* tugged at him until he gave his life to the ministry of the gospel. "Some folks don't believe that God still speaks and ministers to man through His mighty angels, but Brother Don, I sure do. I sure do!"

I was visiting with another pastor friend one day, and we approached the subject of angels. He said, "We as preachers should have discovered the joy of the ministry is praising God. He can make the joy bells ring in His preachers' hearts." I asked him if he had ever seen angels. He smiled and said, "Yes, sir, I have, many times." I asked him to tell me of some of his experiences. "Sometimes," he said, "I get so caught up in the spirit of preaching about sweet Jesus, that while I am preaching it seems like the air is full of angels, beautiful beings. Sometimes it looks like they are inviting me to come on into the kingdom. When that happens, I just can't hold back the tears of joy; my entire soul is flooded with joy. Tears of joy have to come."

With controlled excitement he told me what I already knew. "When God chooses to let you real close to Him, when He gives you a precious glimpse of glory, you can't tell all about it; it just makes you want to weep at His goodness. Yes, He's mighty good, mighty good."

Another pastor friend with whom I play golf and who is also on our Board of Directors told me an incredible story about angels that occurred at his church in Colleyville, Texas. He said, "Several years ago we had a visiting pastor there for revival, and our church had been in much prayer for the crusade." I have preached at this church and am very familiar with the setting. It was built as a large family life center with basketball courts and was easily converted to a worship center accommodating about nine hundred people.

He said that during the revival, on a particular evening, six huge angels appeared in the sanctuary. There were three on the west wall and three on the east wall. "I personally did not see them," he said, "but at least twenty people from the congregation gave me identical reports of what they saw. Six holy angels that must have been thirteen feet tall, clothed in majestic bright, pure white clothes. Their presence created an awesome spiritual peace in the place. While I did not see them, I certainly sensed a holy presence." They appeared; they were visible to many. They disappeared.

I read of two teenage girls walking to their home after a

party. As they talked, they noticed there were some guys following behind them who were making intimidating remarks to them. They were somewhat in the distance, but the girls were feeling very uncomfortable as the boys and their voices got closer. The girls prayed. Suddenly, when they were the most frightened, the boys stopped following and turned the opposite direction.

The next day at school one of the boys came up to the girls and apologized for following them and for the intimidating words. The girl accepted his apology and then asked him why they turned so quickly and went the other direction. "It was those two huge guys walking with you."

One of the girls said, "There was no one with us; we were alone."

The boy replied, "Oh, no, we all saw them. There were two really big guys with you."

I will share one more short story. We have several people who participate in our prison ministry, and we travel to many prisons throughout the United States. We schedule prison services by geographical location. Once we received an invitation to go to a particular facility, we would then schedule other prisons in the general vicinity; it was just the best way to do it. I vividly recall a trip to California that had a gap in the schedule.

We needed a prison in the general area to fill a particular date. It seemed virtually impossible to reach the chaplain by phone. In one of our group prayer meetings I prayed that God would send an angel to help bring about this service. I wrote a letter to the chaplain but did not hear back. The date for us to leave was getting very close when I got a reply from that chaplain inviting us to come.

We arrived and had a very good service at the Reception

Center facility in Tehachapi. I liked the chaplain. I remember over the door to his office it said, "Much Prayer—Much Power." He also said this many times while we were there. After the service he took us back to his office, and we visited briefly. He said, "You know the strangest thing happened with your letter. I put it aside several times over the days, and it seemed to always be back on the center of my desk. It was like an angel kept putting it in front of me." We all looked at each other and smiled; we knew.

So Many Things That Angels Do

Several things are clear about the angels. They belong to God in a unique way. They are not subject to the limitations of time and space. Though they are superhuman, they can and often do assume a recognizable human form. It appears that they come to be in a body form corresponding to the nature of the mission to be fulfilled. Generally, however, it is the human form.

There are many scriptural revelations of angels. Balaam's donkey saw one standing with a drawn sword in Numbers 22:23. In Joshua 5:13 the angel appeared as a man with a sword in his hand carrying an awesome holy presence from God. For one particular assignment angels carried slaughter weapons (Ezek. 9:2). They ride horses and go to and fro on the earth. In Zechariah 1 they expressed God's will to man.

A terrible, destroying angel was sent to do destruction, and would have, except for God's mercy. When David got a glimpse of this angel, he said he "saw the angel of the LORD stand between the earth and the heaven, having a drawn sword in his hand stretched out over Jerusalem" (1 Chron. 21:16). In the Book of Daniel reference is made to an angel "clothed in linen, whose loins were girded with fine gold of Uphaz: His body also was like the beryl, and his face as the appearance of lightning, and his eyes as lamps of fire, and his arms and his feet like in colour to polished brass, and the voice of his words like the voice of a multitude" (Dan. 10:5–6). Angels appear throughout the Old Testament always on a mission from God toward man. They are extraordinary emissaries!

Angels appear to man as the go-between of God's power and will and to execute His dispensations. They are excellent executives. Angels reveal themselves to individuals as well as to whole nations in order to announce events, either good or bad, affecting the people. Not only were they active at announcing the birth of Jesus, but they were also present to foretell to Abraham the birth of Isaac (Gen. 18:10). They showed up again to Abraham to warn of the destruction of Sodom and Gomorrah in Genesis chapters 18 and 19. In Judges 13:3 an angel announces the birth of Samson.

The angels are also protectors of the little children, who always behold the face of the Father. God sent an angel to protect the people after their exodus from Egypt, to lead them to the Promised Land, and to destroy the hostile tribes in their way. Angels are powerful and dreadful, endowed with wisdom and with knowledge of earthly events; they are holy and correct in their judgment, holy, but obviously not infallible.

Jacob meets a host of angels and wrestles with one of the angels (Gen. 32). They are innumerable. Hebrews 12:22 describes the heavenly hosts: "But ye are come unto mount Sion, and unto the city of the living God, the heavenly Jerusalem, and to an innumerable company of angels." Too many to number!

Joshua sees the "captain of the host of the Lord." He appears to Joshua, as we read here:

And it came to pass, when Joshua was by Jericho, that he lifted up his eyes and looked, and, behold, there stood a man over against him with his sword drawn in his hand: and Joshua went unto him, and said unto him, Art thou for us, or for our adversaries? And he said, Nay; but as captain of the host of the LORD am I now come. And Joshua fell on his face to the earth, and did worship, and said unto him, What saith my lord unto his servant? And the captain of the LORD's host said unto Joshua, Loose thy shoe from off thy foot; for the place whereon thou standest is holy. And Joshua did so.

—JOSHUA 5:13–15

Wow, what encounters fill God's Word!

God sits on His throne, and the entire host of heaven stand by Him on His right hand and on His left! Angels are referred to in connection with their special missions, like special agents; for instance, the "angel which hath redeemed," "an interpreter," "the angel that destroyed," "messenger of the covenant," "angel of His presence," and "a band of angels of evil."

After Elijah had encountered the prophets of Baal, he was so mentally and physically drained that he walked for a full day and lay down under a juniper tree wanting to die. He was suicidal. The spiritual battle took so much out of him that he was depressed and felt defeated. Many of us have been there in a sense of speaking, a time when we feel so low after experiencing such highs. God dispatched a special angel to where he was, and the angel touched him and told him to arise and eat (1 Kings 19:5–7).

The angel knew all about Elijah's situation and had doubtlessly been one of the many angels that sustained him through the battle. This angel actually cooked a meal and provided water for the weary saint. It appears that Elijah was so tired that he dozed off again. The angel touched him the second time and explained to him that the journey had been too great for him and that he needed nourishment. Sometimes I ask God's permission to let me thank the angels who minister in my behalf. They do a good job!

There are also defending and destroying angels throughout God's Word. One of my favorite passages is in 2 Kings 19:32–36. In it is recorded the account of one angel destroying 185,000 men of the Assyrian army gathered to conquer Jerusalem. The city was threatened and faced decimation, but God had heard the prayers of His people.

> Therefore thus saith the LORD concerning the king of Assyria, He shall not come into this city, nor shoot an arrow there, nor come before it with shield, nor cast a bank against it. By the way that he came, by the same shall he return, and shall not come into this city, saith the LORD. For I will defend this city, to save it, for mine own sake, and for my servant David's sake. And it came to pass that night, that the angel of the LORD went out, and smote in the camp of the Assyrians an hundred fourscore and five thousand: and when they arose early in the morning, behold, they were all dead corpses. So Sennacherib king of Assyria departed, and went and returned, and dwelt at Nineveh.

God had promised in verse 7 to "send a blast" upon the armies. I live in a city of almost two hundred thousand people. I have often wondered how long it would take one angel to go from house to house to do such destruction. That's a lot of people; that is a huge army. Can you imagine the logistics involved to get such an army from Nineveh to Jerusalem? It is estimated that this army journeyed more than five hundred miles. Horses, tents, water, food—what an undertaking! Now they are outside the city camped for a march against Jerusalem. And God sends one angel.

Some have speculated that the angel used a *simoom* wind to destroy the army. A simoom, which means "poison wind," is a strong, dry, dust-laden wind that blows in the Sahara, Palestine, Israel, Jordan, Syria, and the deserts of the Arabian Peninsula. Its temperature may exceed 129 degrees Fahrenheit, and the humidity may fall below 10 percent. The storm moves in cyclone form, carrying clouds of dust and sand, and the effects on humans and animals are suffocating. The sudden onset of a simoom may also cause heat stroke. This is attributed to the fact that the hot wind brings more heat to the body than can be disposed of by the evaporation of perspiration.

It is most probable that it was this hot south wind, the simoom, the angel used to destroy the Assyrian army. An angel would certainly know how to do it. Even today these unusual winds envelop and destroy whole caravans. Josephus says this angel act was done by a "pestilential" disease, which was instant death to them—no doubt from the "poison wind."[1] One angel that defends and destroys!

I like the way this is described in 2 Kings 19:35–36: "And when they arose early in the morning, behold, they were all dead corpses. So Sennacherib king of Assyria departed, and went and returned, and dwelt at Nineveh." They woke up, and they were all dead—this must indicate that some survived. It just sounds funny when you read it. The king survived, and he said, "I'm getting out of here." He went back to Nineveh. There is no doubt that angels have special assignments.

Chapter 11

ANGELS FROM THE THRONE

IT IS THE angels' job, it is their creative duty and privilege, to worship and glorify God. The highest honor among creation would be to be in God's presence, to be around His very throne, to worship Him. They are the executives. They execute for God. They execute the will of God. You could not help but worship Him in His presence; you could not do anything else than proclaim Him holy.

In the hierarchy of the Highest, the word *seraphim* means, "burning ones or nobles." They are also sometimes called the "ones of love" because their name may come from the Hebrew root for *love*. Seraphim are only fully described in the Bible on one occasion in the Book of Isaiah, chapter 6, when he is being commissioned by God to be a prophet and he has a vision of heaven.

Seraphim have six wings, but they only use two of them for flying. It sounds strange to use wings to cover your face and feet. They may well cover their face because being so close to God and witnessing His full glory would be too powerful to behold. We are not told how many seraphim there are, but it's more than one. Perhaps covering their face and feet is not meant in the sense of hiding, but rather it is the position of their wings.

Seraphim were circling above God's throne, unlike the cherubim who are beside or around it. It seems their primary duty is to constantly glorify and praise God, and they may also be the personal *attendant* angels of God. Their eternal declaration, "Holy, holy, holy is the Lord Almighty; the whole earth is full of his glory," has been used by Jews and Christians for thousands of years.

One of the more common concepts is that angels sing and that there is a heavenly choir. The Bible does not say that angels sing, but I think they do. However, it is not specifically mentioned. If they do, it would be beyond description. Billy Graham said, "Angels belong to a uniquely different dimension of creation that we, limited to the natural order, can scarcely comprehend."[1]

Even as the apostle Paul states when he was allowed a peek into paradise, he could not adequately describe what he saw and heard. He saw things inexpressible and not permissible to tell:

> It is not expedient for me doubtless to glory. I will come to visions and revelations of the Lord. I knew a man in Christ above fourteen years ago, (whether in the body, I cannot tell; or whether out of the body, I cannot tell: God knoweth;) such an one caught up to the third heaven. And I knew such a man, (whether in the body, or out of the body, I cannot tell: God knoweth;) how that he was caught up into paradise, and heard unspeakable words, which it is not lawful for a man to utter.
>
> —2 Corinthians 12:1–4

Most theologians believe this was after Paul was stoned and left for dead in the city of Lystra, and that perhaps it was a near-death experience and he was allowed a glimpse of glory.

I think if *to be absent from the body is to be present with the Lord*, then perhaps being almost absent is to be almost present with the Lord. Regardless, he saw something he was unable to describe. Human language simply cannot explain what is beyond our normal human experience. Read Isaiah's vision and understand that he simply could not put it into human terms:

> In the year that king Uzziah died I saw also the LORD sitting upon a throne, high and lifted up, and his train filled the temple. Above it stood the seraphims: each one had six wings; with twain he covered his face, and with twain he covered his feet, and with twain he did fly. And one cried unto another, and said, Holy, holy, holy, is the LORD of hosts: the whole earth is full of his glory. And the posts of the door moved at the voice of him that cried, and the house was filled with smoke. Then said I, Woe is me! for I am undone; because I am a man of unclean lips, and I dwell in the midst of a people of unclean lips: for mine eyes have seen the King, the LORD of hosts. Then flew one of the seraphims unto me, having a live coal in his hand, which he had taken with the tongs from off the altar: And he laid it upon my mouth, and said, Lo, this hath touched thy lips; and thine iniquity is taken away, and thy sin purged. Also I heard the voice of the Lord, saying, Whom shall I send, and who will go for us? Then said I, Here am I; send me.
>
> —ISAIAH 6:1–8

Isaiah saw the Lord high and lifted up. How did he see Him? Was this a vision? What else could it be? He saw the seraphim encircle God's throne and speak to each other describing God's holiness. I am curious about something here. Why did the angel use a tong to take the live coal from the altar and yet touched the same coal to the lips of Isaiah? Was it too hot to handle? Then how could he apply it to Isaiah's lips?

I believe it was something from the altar intended for man and not for angels. I believe it was a blessing from God's presence for a man willing to be obedient to the Lord. I call it *unique anointing*. Something changes when you have seen the King and yield as His servant. Whatever the angel picked up with tongs was not a fiery live coal as we know it, but it was something special. The angel delivered a unique anointing from God's presence to an ordinary man. They are extraordinary emissaries!

Angel Overview

The first appearance of angels in the Bible is in Genesis 3:24, when Adam and Eve were expelled from the Garden of Eden. God placed cherubim to block the entrance with a flaming sword. In terms of biblical frequency the next appearance was some nineteen hundred years later in Genesis 16:7. That is a long period of time for the heavens to be silent regarding angelic activity. Hagar, the Egyptian servant who bore Ishmael to Abraham, was instructed by an angel to return and submit to her mistress, Sarai.

Abraham was visited by God and two angels in Genesis 18:2, when God informed him of the impending destruction of Sodom and Gomorrah. The same two angels visited Lot and instructed him to escape the city with his family before it was destroyed (Gen. 19:1–11). The angels in this case also displayed supernatural power by blinding the wicked men who were threatening Lot.

Jacob saw a multitude of angels (Gen. 32:1), and he immediately recognized them as the army of God. In the Book of

Genesis there are five mentions of angels in a book that spans two thousand to twenty-five hundred years. Five recorded appearances in twenty-five hundred years. This certainly validates that angel appearances are rare. While their visible manifestations have increased since the coming of Christ, their appearances are not *commonplace*, while it does seem they are much more frequent since Jesus, the knowledge of God's Word, and the application of faith in Christ.

One of the most interesting of angel appearances is in Numbers 22:22, when an angel confronts a disobedient prophet Balaam, but it was the donkey that saw the angel at first. I once heard a preacher say, "Even a jackass can recognize his own master." It was that preacher's message that brought me to the altar to surrender to preach.

As it has always been the desire of Satan to be worshipped, it is also the desire of his fallen angels. However, holy angels refuse to be worshipped (Rev. 22:8–9).

The Bible makes it clear that when angels appear, those who see them are often struck with fear (Judg. 6:22; 1 Chron. 21:30; Matt 28:5). They appear, do their job, and then they disappear. Angels deliver messages from God and do His bidding, sometimes by supernatural means. In all situations the angels direct people to God and His will and always give the glory to Him.

There are many modern reports. Angelic visitations come in a variety of forms. In some cases a stranger prevents serious injury or death and then mysteriously disappears. In other cases a winged or white-clothed being is seen momentarily and is then gone. The person who sees the angel is often left with a feeling of peace and assurance of God's presence.

People who describe this type of visitation have some biblical support from Paul's shipwreck experience in Acts 27:22–25 (NKJV):

And now I urge you to take heart, for there will be no loss of life among you, but only of the ship. For there stood by me this night an angel of the God to whom I belong and whom I serve, saying, "Do not be afraid, Paul; you must be brought before Caesar; and indeed God has granted you all those who sail with you." Therefore take heart, men, for I believe God that it will be just as it was told me.

Another type of visitation that I have experienced and heard about often is heaven's music, the *angel choir* type. Luke tells us that the shepherds were visited by what seems to be a heavenly choir as they were told of the birth of Jesus. However, the Bible does not say *choir*; it says "heavenly host."

Now there were in the same country shepherds living out in the fields, keeping watch over their flock by night. And behold, an angel of the Lord stood before them, and the glory of the Lord shone around them, and they were greatly afraid. Then the angel said to them, "Do not be afraid, for behold, I bring you good tidings of great joy which will be to all people. For there is born to you this day in the city of David a Savior, who is Christ the Lord. And this will be the sign to you: You will find a Babe wrapped in swaddling cloths, lying in a manger." And suddenly there was with the angel a multitude of the heavenly host praising God and saying: "Glory to God in the highest, and on earth peace, goodwill toward men!"

—LUKE 2:8–14, NKJV

I find it almost curious that the Bible does not say that the angels sing. They were praising God here, and while personally I believe they do sing, the Bible does not say so. Some people have reported similar experiences in places of worship. This experience is not typical of the angels' interaction with man, but generally those who experience this have a spiritual elation that often signals a new direction toward God. The angel choir in Luke's Gospel was heralding some very specific news.

A third type of visitation involves a physical and deeply spiritual feeling. Elderly people have often reported feeling as though arms or wings were wrapped around them in times of extreme loneliness. God is certainly the God of all comfort, and Scripture speaks of God covering with His wings (Ps. 91:4). Such reports may well be examples of that covering. Recently, through tears, a pastor friend of mine told me of a similar experience where he felt as though God had taken him on His lap and embraced him with love.

Hebrews 13:2 says, "Be not forgetful to entertain strangers: for thereby some have entertained angels unawares." God is still as active in the world as He has always been; He is the same yesterday, today, and forever; and His angels are certainly still at work. Just as angels protected God's people in the past, we can be assured that they are guarding us today. As we obey God's commands, it is quite possible that we may encounter His angels even if we do not realize it. In special circumstances God allowed His people to see His *unseen angels* so God's people would be encouraged and continue in His service (2 Kings 6:16–17). Always it is true that as we are faithful to God, there are more that are with us than are against us.

Isn't it encouraging that we can know that God's angels are at work? In special situations we might even have one of those rare personal visitations. Jesus, who made the angels and receives their worship, has promised us His own presence in our trials. Jesus Himself has said, "Surely I am with you always, to the very end of the age" (Matt. 28:20, NIV).

A few years ago a friend said to me, "I asked the Lord how many angels were assigned to you." He said this in conversation about the deliverance ministry. "You must really stir up activity in the heavens," he said. I told him things were already stirred up in the heavenly realm and that demonic activity is not a new thing. He agreed.

I asked him what the Lord told him in response to his question. "He told me that you had more than a thousand angels assigned to you."

"Is that all?" I said with a smile. Pretty interesting! He is a Baptist deacon and very aware of demons and their works. And he also understands that God has promised His protection and comfort through the ministry of His holy angels. I don't think too much about the numbers, but I am always aware that the name of Jesus is sufficient, and God is way ahead of me on all things going on.

Chapter 12

ANGELIC ACTIVITY SURROUNDING
THE BIRTH OF JESUS

THE TIME HAD come for the greatest announcement of human history. The long-awaited Messiah was to be born of a woman. God's Son was about to lay aside His heavenly garments to take upon Himself the form of a man and to be born of a woman. Someone had to announce to the people that Jesus was coming; a *forerunner* had to tell the people that the King was on His way. God sent an angel to tell man the message that was to be delivered.

Luke's account tells us that the priest Zacharias was in the temple performing his priestly duties when, without warning, "there appeared unto him an angel of the Lord" (Luke 1:11). Zacharias was frightened, for without any prior knowledge or expectation God's angel appeared unto him. Zacharias saw him! The angel calmed him, saying, "Fear not." As you read this account in Luke 2, note these things that happened:

1. Zacharias was in the temple serving God (v. 8).

2. He had prayed. God sent an angel to answer his prayer (v. 13).

3. The angel told of future events (v. 13).

4. The angel brought the name for the child (v. 13).

5. Zacharias saw the angel (v. 12).

6. He conversed with him (v. 18). He questioned him.

7. The angel identified himself (v. 19).

8. The angel pronounced judgment because of Zacharias's doubt (v. 20).

What can be concluded? The angel moved as God commanded, and it was in response to Zacharias's prayer to be used of God. When angels come to man, they come from God's presence. They bring some of that presence with them. In this case the angel also had discretion to exercise judgment. I believe they still have some holy discretion to execute judgment or to bring blessings. For at least nine months Zacharias could not speak, just as the angel had pronounced. In verses 63 and 64, when the child was born, Zacharias was enabled to speak, and he named the child as directed by God's holy angel. The angel appeared, spoke, pronounced judgment, and then disappeared.

God's marvelous messengers were busy as the time drew near. Six months after Gabriel was sent to Zacharias, he was dispatched from the presence of God to a woman named Mary to announce the miraculous birth of God's Son (Luke 1:26). The angels are extraordinary emissaries!

Again we see a hint of the angels' workings. Gabriel goes unannounced to Nazareth, to the home of Mary. He appears and greets her with a message from God's throne. Like Zacharias, Mary was also afraid (v. 29), but as with Zacharias, Mary was told, "Fear not." Just as God sent the name for John,

He did for Jesus (v. 31). Once more let us learn something from this angelic experience in Luke's first chapter.

1. Gabriel was sent (v. 26).

2. He appeared suddenly (v. 28).

3. He spoke (v. 28).

4. Mary saw him (v. 29).

5. Her fear was turned to comfort (v. 30).

6. Future events were revealed unto her (vv. 30–33).

7. She questioned him (v. 34).

8. She received an assuring answer (v. 35).

9. She was given news of Zacharias and Elizabeth (v. 36).

10. The angel proclaimed, "For with God nothing shall be impossible" (v. 37).

And as in other cases throughout the Scriptures, the angel departed from Mary (v. 38). It seems that in a fleeting moment the angels can descend from God's presence, deliver His message, and return. Billy Graham said, "Angels speak. They appear and reappear."[1]

Additionally God had not forgotten about Joseph. Would he believe as Mary had when she told him of the message sent by an angel—that the Holy Spirit would conceive in her and she would be the mother of God's Son? Would you? Joseph was a just man (Matt. 1:19), and knowing Mary was pregnant, he was still prepared to take her as his wife, but surely his mind and heart were troubled. "But while he thought on these things, behold, the angel of the Lord appeared unto him in a dream" (v. 20). Was he awake? Was this a vision or a visitation as Mary and Zacharias had? Notice that verse 24 indicates Joseph was asleep. The angel of the Lord appeared in a dream. Let's look closer:

1. Joseph was troubled before the angel came (Matt. 1:19–20).

2. God knew this and dispatched "the angel of the Lord," who, in this case, remained nameless (v. 20).

3. Joseph was given a heavenly message (v. 20).

4. He was told what to name the child (v. 21).

5. He was assured that this experience was in keeping with the Scripture (vv. 22–23). The angels never speak contradictorily or contrary to God's written Word.

6. Joseph also had assurance from heaven (v. 24).

There is more we can learn from the angels' activity when the Savior of man was born. (Remember, Jesus did not die for fallen angels but for fallen man.) To learn more about fallen angels, read my other books on demons and deliverance, but now let's take a glimpse at their activity here by way of speculation.[2]

There are two classes of angels: God's holy angels, who cannot fall or fail, and those angels who, by their choice, fell in Lucifer's rebellion against the Almighty (Isa. 14:12). They too were busy as the baby Jesus was born, working in the hearts of sinful man. What caused Herod to be troubled when he received news of Jesus's birth? What caused him to want to destroy God's Son (Matt. 2:3–13)?

The fear that came upon Pharaoh when Moses (Israel's deliverer) was born now came upon King Herod. The fallen angels, Satan's host of evil spirits, were seeking to destroy Jesus. However, God intervened and dispatched a messenger to warn Joseph and Mary of impending danger: "The angel of the Lord appeared to Joseph in a dream, saying, Arise, and take the young child and his mother, and flee into Egypt…until I bring thee word" (Matt. 2:13).

God's Son was safe. He was not waiting for heaven to send instructions. As promised, an angel of the Lord appeared in a dream and gave explicit instructions that led Jesus, Joseph, and Mary to Nazareth in Galilee to fulfill the Scripture (vv. 19–23). Much can be learned from this account. What has happened? An apparent spiritual confrontation of God's holy angels and Satan's fallen angels. God's angels cannot fail because they are God's angels. They are superior because He is! Look at their activities in Matthew, chapter 2:

1. The angels warned of danger (v. 13).

2. The angels directed them from danger (v. 13).

3. The angels left a promise—"until I bring thee word" (v. 13).

4. The angels kept their promise (v. 19).

5. The angels could not act contrary to Scripture (vv. 22–23).

6. The angels in Joseph's life always appeared "in a dream."

7. There is no indication that Joseph had conversations with the angels or questioned the angels; he only obeyed these heavenly messengers.

8. Angels are mentioned five times in Matthew's account of Joseph (Matt. 1:20, 24; 2:13, 19, 22). Each came with a message from God.

Matthew and Luke record the birth and childhood of Jesus. Possibly the most complete account is found in Luke 2. Luke reminds us that angels not only dealt with priests in the temple, with the chosen mother of Jesus, and with Joseph her espoused, but they also appeared to shepherds who were watching over their flocks by night (vv. 9–15). The glory of the angels was so bright, so magnificent, that the shepherds were afraid. The angel, as directed by God, spoke that great verse of Scripture so often quoted at Christmas time: "For unto you is born this day in the city of David a Savior, which is Christ the Lord" (v. 11).

Something can be learned from this angelic visitation.

1. The angel appeared to more than one individual (v. 8).

2. The angel brought with him some of God's presence (v. 9).

3. The angel appeared unexpectedly, but he characteristically calmed those to whom he appeared. "Fear not" (v. 10).

4. The angel brought only a heavenly message (vv. 11–12).

5. "Suddenly" there appeared with the angel a multitude of angels (v. 13).

6. The host of angels came unannounced, performing their heavenly duty of "praising God."

7. Their mission accomplished, they were gone. They appeared. They spoke. They disappeared.

They appear. They do their job. They disappear.

Somewhere, sometime, in the predeterminate counsel of God the Father, Son, and Holy Spirit, there was agreement to create a vast host of angelic beings. The holy agreement was to do this "by Jesus and for Jesus." I would like to tell you why and how this came about, but I don't know, nor does anyone else. We know only what is revealed through God's Word, so we do know that the angels were created by Jesus and for Jesus: "All things were made by him; and without him was not anything made that was made" (John 1:3).

The apostle Paul confirms this:

> For by him were all things created, that are in heaven, and that are in earth, visible and invisible, whether they be thrones, or dominions, or principalities, or powers: all things were created by him, and for him: And he is before all things, and by him all things consist.
> —Colossians 1:16–17

Further, Paul wrote about Jesus and His position in the heavenly places, saying:

> That ye may know what is the hope of his calling, and what the riches of the glory of his inheritance in the saints, and what is the exceeding greatness of his power to usward who believe, according to the working of

his mighty power, which he wrought in Christ, when he raised him from the dead, and set him at his own right hand in the heavenly places, far above all principality, and power, and might, and dominion, and every name that is named, not only in this world, but also in that which is to come: and hath put all things under his feet, and gave him to be the head over all things to the church, which is his body, the fulness of him that filleth all in all.

—EPHESIANS 1:18–23

Thrones, dominions, might, principalities, or powers—they were all created by Jesus. Generally, when talking about principalities and powers, we think about demon powers. But first there were only angelic powers. Their sophisticated hierarchy and governmental operations were all established by God through Jesus.

While it is amazingly vast, we are part of it. If you remove people from the equation, there is no warfare as we know it in the heavenly realm. It's all about people. God so loved the world because of the people. Demons don't want a tree in Iowa; there's no contention there, so it's all about people. Knowing what little we know about God's amazing universe, it seems we are at the center of it all. I don't know about you, but I am very humbled that God is mindful of me!

Chapter 13

DO ANGELS BRING HEALING?

Without doubt, in the fifth chapter of John is one of the most curious passages in the New Testament.

> After this there was a feast of the Jews, and Jesus went up to Jerusalem. Now there is in Jerusalem by the Sheep Gate a pool, which is called in Hebrew, Bethesda, having five porches. In these lay a great multitude of sick people, blind, lame, paralyzed, waiting for the moving of the water. For an angel went down at a certain time into the pool and stirred up the water; then whoever stepped in first, after the stirring of the water, was made well of whatever disease he had. Now a certain man was there who had an infirmity thirty-eight years. When Jesus saw him lying there, and knew that he already had been in that condition a long time, He said to him, "Do you want to be made well?"
>
> The sick man answered Him, "Sir, I have no man to put me into the pool when the water is stirred up; but while I am coming, another steps down before me." Jesus said to him, "Rise, take up your bed and walk." And immediately the man was made well, took up his bed, and walked. And that day was the Sabbath. The Jews therefore said to him who was cured, "It is the Sabbath;

it is not lawful for you to carry your bed." He answered them, "He who made me well said to me, 'Take up your bed and walk.'"

Then they asked him, "Who is the Man who said to you, 'Take up your bed and walk'?" But the one who was healed did not know who it was, for Jesus had withdrawn, a multitude being in that place. Afterward Jesus found him in the temple, and said to him, "See, you have been made well. Sin no more, lest a worse thing come upon you." The man departed and told the Jews that it was Jesus who had made him well.

—JOHN 5:1–15, NKJV

This *healing pool* is full of mystery. Did an angel really come and stir the water? Skeptics even doubted the existence of the pool until fifty or so years ago. The Romans had so completely destroyed Herod's Jerusalem that the pool could not be found. Now archaeologists have unearthed this pool, and only skeptics doubt what happened at the pool.[1] I see great truth in this account at the *Mercy Pool*. (*Bethesda* means, "House of Mercy.")

Running hot springs filled the pool. Some say the sick came because of the healing minerals in the water. There were many sick people at this site. The Bible says a "great multitude" with all kinds of sicknesses. It wasn't getting into the water that brought the healing—it was getting in first after an angel stirred the waters.

That Jesus comes by at this appointed time is hope for us all. I'm sure the man who had been lain daily at the pool had prayed many, many times. He was older than Jesus and had suffered his lame condition for thirty-eight years! I'm guessing the man was more than fifty years old. Apparently the man's lifestyle caused his problem—as we see in verse 14: "See, you have been made well. Sin no more, lest a worse thing come upon you" (NKJV). In other words, Jesus was saying, "Next time it could be worse!"

When Jesus asked the man if he would like to be healed, it seemed a strange question. What He did was give the man an opportunity to confess—blessing starts with confessing! When the man admitted he could not get healed without the help of someone else, Jesus told him, "Rise, take up thy bed, and walk" (v. 8). Confessing precedes blessing! The first step in gaining victory with God is to *admit* that you need it. The man did not even know who Jesus was. He did know that it was by the power of God that he had received healing. He went to the temple immediately afterward, undoubtedly to give thanks.

There he bumps into Jesus, and Jesus said to him: "Behold, thou art made whole: sin no more, lest a worse thing come unto thee" (v. 14). Amazing! Jesus said that his sickness was directly related to his sin: "Don't do this anymore; next time it might be worse. Quit it!" This is unmistakably what Jesus said and what the Word teaches. Admit it and quit it!

Admit It and Quit It

In Psalm 107:17 we read, "Fools because of their transgression, and because of their iniquities, are afflicted." The Revised Standard Version states it like this: "Some were sick through their sinful ways, and because of their iniquities suffered affliction."

Someone asked me one day what this man could have done to bring about his sickness. I don't know, nor does anyone else. However, there are many things that it could have been, including the possibility of sexual promiscuousness. There are many famous people who died because of their lifestyles—Napoleon Bonaparte is one. He conquered and ruled over much of western and central Europe. Napoleon was one of the so-called "enlightened monarchs." It is suspected that he suffered from syphilis and probably died from it.[2] Sexually transmitted diseases are rampant today, and they all carry a physical penalty.

Whatever may have been the source of sin for this man at the pool of Bethesda, he was told, "Don't do it anymore—the results may be worse next time." Stop it and drop it! Confess it and address it! Abstain and refrain. You can't be free from something if you keep doing the thing that gives permission—legal rights—to demons.

Once you are made whole, the goal is to remain whole! Admit it, quit it, and submit it! You must submit your flesh, your lifestyle, to God. There must be submission. That involves your will and desire. There must be surrender. Doors that were openings for demon powers to bring sickness and other areas of darkness must be closed.

Submission is a choice, and only you can make it. A deliverance minister can't make it for you, and your spouse or parents can't do it for you; it is a conscious choice that only you can make. In this case surrender is a choice that will bring victory. Sometimes preachers, teachers, or religious views can complicate a very simple truth. I hope this helps to make things less complicated.

Accepting God's great forgiveness, for some reason, is difficult for a lot of people. Even after confession some want to *feel* guilty because of their sin. Forgiveness is what God does, and it is based upon our confession, not what we feel like. Feel forgiven because you *are* forgiven! Receiving God's forgiveness is a done deal. Don't keep bringing up your past, which is forgiven and has been cleansed. It gives advantage to demons. Admit it, quit it, submit it, and forget it.

It's not any more difficult than that. God remembers our sins no more! What's important, then, is that *we* remember them no more. What God has forgiven is forgiven. The sooner we learn to walk in this simple truth, the quicker we can realize the freedom promised.

Living under the unnecessary condemnation of yesterday really means we have not fully realized His great forgiveness. So far as the east is from the west He has removed our sin from us. If He forgets it, you forget it. Condemnation is not God's way. Forgiven? Forget it!

Unfortunately there is not much talk today about God's supernatural healing. However, it is a part of the atonement and very clearly taught in the Scriptures. An angel brought healing to Elijah through natural means. He cooked him a meal and nourished him through food, drink, and rest. Angels, without doubt, assist doctors and researchers in the medical field. They enlighten and guide surgeons' hands.

One of the things I have found to be puzzling is how demon powers are able to twist Scripture to their advantage. They attempt to convince people that their *sickness* is sent by God, and since God didn't heal Paul's thorn in the flesh, He will not heal them either. "And lest I should be exalted above measure through the abundance of the revelations, there was given to me a thorn in the flesh, the messenger of Satan to buffet me, lest I should be exalted above measure" (2 Cor. 12:7).

For generations Bible commentators have offered countless theories as to what Paul's thorn in the flesh was. The most popular theories for Paul's malady range from various and sundry illnesses, such as malaria, epilepsy, or eye disease, to a haunting guilt for persecuting the church; some say it was a sexual addiction that Paul never got victory over—all of which are just speculation.

Clearly the Bible states that it was a "messenger of Satan," a demon power sent (allowed) to harass or buffet him. It may have been a sickness, but the Bible does not say so. Paul was persecuted wherever he went and suffered the consequences of the persecutions. God's grace being sufficient for him is not the same as saying, "Well, I guess God wants me sick to bring Him glory." What a ridiculous theology that is.

I was taking a lady through deliverance in Oklahoma a few years ago. She resisted a bit when I was dealing with her sickness. She said, "I believe the Lord is trying to show me something through this sickness."

I remember saying to her, "Ma'am, you are seventy-eight years old; what do you think He's trying to show you?" I said this kindly of course, and she ultimately agreed that God was not the source of her sickness.

However, people get sick. Much of Jesus's ministry was healing the sick. I believe angels are very active in ministering to the sick and in bringing healing. Look at the various ways that healing can come.

> Is any sick among you? let him call for the elders of the church; and let them pray over him, anointing him with oil in the name of the Lord: and the prayer of faith shall save the sick, and the Lord shall raise him up; and if he have committed sins, they shall be forgiven him. Confess your faults one to another, and pray one for another, that ye may be healed. The effectual fervent prayer of a righteous man availeth much.
>
> —James 5:14–16

The elders of the church can anoint individuals with oil, pray for them, and they may be healed. Perhaps you are someone who has been healed through this scriptural obedient act of faith. Are angels involved here?

The Bible tells us that people can be healed by way of God's people casting out demons and by the laying on of hands on each other in prayer. This seems to be more of a work of the Holy Spirit, but angels possibly assist.

> And these signs shall follow them that believe; In my name shall they cast out devils...they shall lay hands on the sick, and they shall recover.
>
> —MARK 16:17–18

Remarkably I have seen hundreds healed by casting out devils. Many, many times the demons are the source of the sickness. In my experience healing more often comes through the casting out of the sickness and the demons that were causing it than through the laying on of hands.

God may grant some the gift of healing with authority to minister healing to others. This is mentioned in 1 Corinthians 12:9: "To another faith by the same Spirit; to another the gifts of healing by the same Spirit." It seems obvious that not every believer has every gift of the Spirit. God decides, and God divides the gifts. However, some have the gift of healing, and their prayer can bring healing. In many respects medical doctors fall into this category.

God may grant healing in response to the faith of the person who desires healing. For some reason there is spiritual boasting in this area: "Well, I don't take any medicine, and I'm fit as a fiddle." I know you've heard that. Taking or not taking medicine does not make you any closer to God. He is always the healer. It is by His great mercy and love that healing comes.

Healing is often administered by the angels, and demons are virtually always the source of the need for healing.

> But Jesus turned him about, and when he saw her, he said, Daughter, be of good comfort; thy faith hath made thee whole. And the woman was made whole from that hour.
>
> —MATTHEW 9:22

While faith may always be a factor, in this case it is *the* factor. Jesus clearly said, "Your faith has made you whole." It was her faith and her actions based upon her faith! Jesus responds to faith. God is a God of faith.

However, there are other examples of God healing someone on behalf of the faith of others, as we saw in one example earlier.

> And when they could not come nigh unto him for the press, they uncovered the roof where he was: and when they had broken it up, they let down the bed wherein the sick of the palsy lay. When Jesus saw their faith, he said unto the sick of the palsy, Son, thy sins be forgiven thee.
>
> —MARK 2:4–5

This should always be an encouragement for believers to pray for and believe for others. Though faith again is an issue, Jesus acted upon the faith of others.

God often heals through medical treatment.

> Drink no longer water, but use a little wine for thy stomach's sake and thine often infirmities.
>
> —1 TIMOTHY 5:23

> But a certain Samaritan, as he journeyed, came where he was: and when he saw him, he had compassion on him,

and went to him, and bound up his wounds, pouring in
oil and wine, and set him on his own beast, and brought
him to an inn, and took care of him.

—LUKE 10:33–34

One of my favorites is the account of King Hezekiah in
2 Kings 20:7: "And Isaiah said, Take a lump of figs. And they
took and laid it on the boil, and he recovered."
Even after the miracle of his prayer for more life and added
days, Hezekiah still needed healing. Does it seem like God
would have just spoken His healing when He added His days
of life to Hezekiah? God ordered him a prescription, and
Isaiah became his doctor and pharmacist. I think most of us
have experienced healing through the hands of a medical professional. It is no less of a miracle. I am just as grateful to God
regardless of the method of the healing.

There is an additional way of healing in Scripture. God
performs sovereign acts of mercy to heal. He takes the initia-
tive; He does the work. We have already seen this example of
healing in the experience of the man at the pool of Bethesda
in John 5:2–9.

This is an incredible act of God's mercy. I'm certain this
man had prayed, and I feel certain that others had prayed for
him, but in this case Jesus just stopped by! The man wanted
healing and had some expectation of it. Perhaps he had done
all he knew to do. Sometimes healing comes as a sovereign
act of God's mercy and grace. The common denominator is
always Jesus. He's the healer!

John Calvin, when a pastor and young reformer, said:

> Angels are the ministers and dispensers of the divine
> bounty towards us. Accordingly, we are told how they
> watch for our safety, how they undertake our defence,

direct our path, and take heed that no evil befall us. There are whole passages which relate, in the first instance, to Christ, the Head of the Church, and after him to all believers. "He shall give his angels charge over thee, to keep thee in all thy ways. They shall bear thee up in their hands, lest thou dash thy foot against a stone." Again, "The angel of the Lord encampeth round about them that fear him, and delivereth them." By these passages the Lord shows that the protection of those whom he has undertaken to defend he has delegated to his angels.[3]

Angels doubtless are involved in bringing about God's mercy in acts of healing. As you read these scriptural truths, I pray you are encouraged and that your faith is stirred to some action. I, by faith, pray healing for everyone who reads these words.

Chapter 14

WHAT ANGELS ARE NOT

ANGELS ARE NOT some kind of feminine creature with bowed heads and strange looks upon their faces. The Bible gives no indication of angels being feminine but rather implies they are masculine, as we understand masculinity. They are powerful. They appear throughout Scripture in the form of men. They bear names of men—for example, Michael, Gabriel.

The angels are not *saints who have died*! Somewhere in man's thinking this seemed to be an appealing thought, but again, it is contrary to Scripture. Christians do not become angels. They receive a glorified body and will ever serve the Lord as His redeemed, blood-bought creation: "We shall be like him" (1 John 3:2).

Husbands who refer to their wives as angels do so as a compliment and term of endearment. No man with an understanding of Scripture wants an angel for a wife. They are non-feminine, powerful, nonreproductive, and always right.

I have yet to find a scripture that describes the halo all angels traditionally have. They do have an aura, or a spiritual glow from God's presence. Whether or not they have halos is not really important. It is important that we put aside all that is not in God's Word. His Word will be true to us. His Spirit will give us understanding as we seek to know more about His

144

holy creatures. Make sure the Holy Word of God justifies the faith that you have placed in religious tradition.

Angels are not all alike. Their descriptions throughout the sixty-six books of God's Word are many and varied; they are mentioned sixty-six times in the Book of Revelation alone. They do not all have the same power. Angels are not funny-looking, little chubby, red-faced babies with wings. Man has somehow chosen to picture this silly-looking little creature as the biblical cherub. No!

The cherubim (plural) were placed as guards at the Garden of Eden with flaming swords. The Bible gives no account of fat little baby angels. The angels are immortal; in other words, they will live forever. Therefore they are not aged. They do not desire man's worship. They are not emotionless robots. Some willingly rebelled against God. They are not without freedom of choice. This is evident just in the fact of fallen angels. Any believer with an inkling of Bible knowledge knows that God did not create anything bad. At one time there were only holy angels. For some reason, a host of angels rebelled against God.

Some angels have fallen, as many say. But I believe *fallen* is too weak of a word to describe what happened. They didn't *fall* out of heaven. They were kicked out, cast down to the earth. Lucifer was the leader of these rebels. God created them with choice, and our only reason for discussing this now is to understand that angels are not *puppets* of God. They are not machinelike creatures, but they do move at His direction.

Angels are not omniscient, and they do not have full knowledge of God's plan and program. They are intelligent beings, but they are finite. The attribute of omniscience belongs only to God. God apparently created them to share in His counsel and wisdom, for they help carry out the plan and will of

God. Still, it is important to remember that their intelligence, though greater than man's, is limited.

Angels are not able to act without God's direction. This is an assumption well supported by Scripture. They move as His messengers, His holy deputies, at His command.

We can be sure of this: the fallen angels can never be holy angels again, just as the rich man could not return from hell. The fallen angels are in "chains of darkness, to be reserved unto judgment" (2 Pet. 2:4). First Corinthians 6:3 indicates that Christians will judge angels—not the holy angels, but the fallen angels that sinned against God. The angels are not our servants; they are God's!

They are "ministering spirits, sent forth to minister for them who shall be heirs of salvation" (Heb. 1:14). Yes, angels minister *for believers*, not *to* them, but only as they are *sent forth* from God. (The angels are not bodily in form, though they may take on such form.) They are spirits and fit in the realm of the invisible principalities and powers. Jesus clearly gave us authority in "loosing and binding" spirits. I believe that includes authority in the name of Jesus Christ not only to bind evil spirits, but to also release and receive holy angels to minister for us.

Angels do not obey man, and they cannot intercede in prayer. Jesus is our intercessor! Angels may come to answer the prayers of believers, but only as directed by God. They do not desire any of the glory that belongs to God.

The Angels Are Not Gone

Perhaps you expect to read somewhere in here that angels are not active today, that their earthly ministry ended somewhere in times past. Oh, no, quite the opposite! When the fires of persecution and martyrdom flamed around God's children, believers related stories of angels intervening. However, in today's age of plenty, we have become less dependent upon God. We have become educated enough to rationalize the supernatural and, to some degree, to pride ourselves on being self-sufficient. Sadly we do not look for, nor do we expect, the ministry of angels. Faith has dwindled as man's knowledge has increased; as luxury came, so did independence from God. God has not changed, nor will He! The angels have not changed! Their creative purpose is the same. The assignments given them by Jehovah God have not changed. We have!

The angels are not gone! They stand ready to minister. Of all the things they are not, they are not gone!

Satan and his demon powers have made an attack upon every biblical doctrine, his purpose being to deceive or confuse believers or potential believers. Giving credit where credit is due, Satan has done a good job of confusing man concerning God's supernatural creation. As he has done with salvation, he has split believers into groups called denominations, many denominations, that take the same Bible and teach doctrines of error as truth. Satan can transform himself as an angel of light, and he has his *own* messengers in the pulpits (2 Cor. 11:13–14). So it is not surprising that belief about angels is as wide and as varied as denominationalism itself.

If Satan could deceive the *elect of God*, he would have you disregard *his* fallen angels and God's holy angels. He would have you *explain away* the supernatural. In our brilliance we can also be astoundingly stupid. Why are we more ready to doubt than to believe? Should God not be praised?

I recently spoke at length with a hospital chaplain. I questioned him concerning angels in his ministry. He told me of a man who was clinically dead because of a cardiac arrest. The blood was not moving through the man's body, and his heart was not working. After about three minutes, the chaplain explained, the doctors succeeded in reviving the man.

The chaplain told me that the man, though his mind and body were clinically dead, had heard every word spoken by the doctors and attendants while they frantically worked to bring life back to his body.

He also said he saw his mother and father (long before deceased) standing at the foot of his bed. He further stated that he did not want to *come back*. He had seen something so beautiful and peaceful that he wanted to *go on in*. "The mother and father at the foot of his bed...," I asked, "how do you explain that? Were they really angels in the form of his mother and father?" The chaplain responded by saying, "I really don't know how to explain it. It may have been his deceased parents already in heaven and he got a glimpse of them, and it may have been angels."

The angels of God were sent to escort Lazarus into paradise! However, this man did not go to paradise; he did not die! I will use the chaplain's words: "I really don't know how to explain it." Would angels appear to frighten a dying man? Of course not! The angels of God would appear to comfort a dear saint, to assure him. The man was fully aware of every word spoken, every movement and action taken in the room while he was clinically dead. I believe God allowed this man a glimpse of glory. My personal opinion in this given situation is that angels took on a recognizable form and ministered to this dying saint who did not die. And then again, the dying man may have been so on the edge of death that he saw into the spirit realm.

To *slip out* of this body may be to *slip into* the edge of eternity. There are numerous accounts of similar visions in time of death and danger. Now let me be quick to say, modernists would have you logically analyze this and call it hallucination or tricks of the mind. Let me urge you to spiritually and scripturally examine such experiences and to recognize that this is not contrary to Scripture. Stephen, while dying, said, "I see Jesus." (See Acts 7:55–60.)

Stories of dying lost men are just as numerous, but the opposite is true in their release from this life. One hospital spokesman told me of cries of: "No, someone help me!" "Don't let me leave this body." Some have described visions of snakes and spiders. Does Satan send his mongrels for the unbelievers? "The rich man also died, and was buried; and in hell…" (Luke 16:22–23).

It is clear that the angels of God are not *visibly* sent to everyone. Angelic activity increased as the birth of Jesus neared. This is true because millions and millions of believers have never seen or heard an angel. This does nothing to disprove their ministry, nor does it discredit God's Word. It is a reflection upon man's complete faith in the supernatural God. There is no activity of God apart from His Spirit. "God is a Spirit: and they that worship him must worship him in spirit and in truth" (John 4:24).

The holy angels are a part of God's holy creation, man is a part of His redemptive creation, and faith joins the two. Just as man believes in God by faith, as he accepts His Word by faith, he accepts the reality of angels by faith.

Unholy man is joined to our holy God by the redemptive work of Jesus. As the redeemed of God and an heir of salvation, I have holy angels ministering for me—not because I am holy, but because He is holy and I am His. Let me repeat again: there are many things that angels are not, but they are not gone! The liberal or the slow in faith might call heavenly revelation "hallucination." He hurts himself! Bible wisdom and spiritual discernment are imperative as we experience the supernatural.

God's angels are alive and well, working in the lives of believers. The angels are not gone! Perhaps this is an inconclusive statement. If they are not gone, where are they? Remember, angels are spirits; they are not visible to the human eye. However, angels are not limited to just an *invisible spiritual existence*. If God so chooses, an angel can appear in a form recognizable to man. Human eyes do not often perceive the presence of angels in the majority of cases. As ministering spirits (Heb. 1:14) they are not visible. The exception is rare, extremely rare, in our daily work. You can talk with thousands of Christians and never meet one who has seen an angel, though most all believers can tell you of an experience that involved angels.

Angels Are Different From Humans

Let us look further at what angels are not. By having angels compared with believers, there are few similarities. The angels cannot call God *Father* as a believer does, for we know God the Father through redemption. We have sinned; the holy angels have not, and thus they have no need of salvation. Jesus did not die for the angels. They know God as their Creator and Master but not as God who gave His only begotten Son for them.

The angels are not filled or indwelt by the Holy Spirit; again the distinction is made by relationship to God. The Holy Spirit is God! Jesus promised His presence to believers only. Since the angels are not born again, they are not indwelt with the

Holy Spirit. However, they are subject to the Spirit's direction in that the Holy Spirit is God in the third person.

The angels don't know the future unless God reveals it to them. Jesus confirmed this truth when He said in Matthew 24:36–39:

> But of that day and hour knoweth no man, no, not the angels of heaven, but my Father only. But as the days of Noah were, so shall also the coming of the Son of man be. For as in the days that were before the flood they were eating and drinking, marrying and giving in marriage, until the day that Noe entered into the ark, and knew not until the flood came, and took them all away; so shall also the coming of the Son of man be.

There seems to be a strong emphasis by Jesus concerning the angels and their abilities when He says "not even the angels"—almost as if He were saying, "They know a lot about God, they are magnificent messengers, but not even the angels know the hour of My coming."

The angels are not heirs of God, or heirs of salvation. They are not joint heirs with Jesus Christ. The angels are not going to share in our inheritance. Heaven comes to the believer, again, because of redemption. Angels have not had this experience. Furthermore, they cannot have this experience. The angels cannot even bear personal witness of salvation. The privilege of sharing Jesus's redemptive death and resurrection is denied to the angels. They can rejoice at His coming, at His resurrection, His ascension and return, but while they are certainly aware, they have not experienced sin and rebirth. They can and do rejoice when man receives Jesus, but angels cannot bear personal witness of salvation by experience.

Angels are not confined to heaven and earth. This earth is

not the only place inhabited by angels. Out there in the vastness of infinity, beyond the comprehension of the human mind, beyond our ability to grasp, there are ministering spirits called the angels of God.

Jesus said, "Likewise, I say unto you, there is joy in the presence of angels of God over one sinner that repenteth" (Luke 15:10). They are everywhere and in close contact with the events of heaven and earth. Angels are in heaven worshipping and praising God, and just as surely angels are ministering for the saints here on earth. Remember they are not ministering to us but for us! Much more could be written about what angels are not, but the greatest truth I can leave you with is that they most certainly are not gone!

Angel Misinformation

Do we have guardian angels? The Bible doesn't give a definitive answer on that, but clearly that is a function that angels may have. I personally believe that we do. Psalm 91:11 promises: "For he shall give his angels charge over thee, to keep thee in all thy ways." There are thousands of stories about angels that protected and rescued people, both Christians and non-Christians. But nagging questions continue to arise: Where are the angels when girls are raped? When drunk drivers crash headlong into a car of teenagers? When evil people blow up buildings with hundreds of innocent people in them?

The angels are still there, continuing to minister in pain and death. We obviously don't realize the role of angels in the midst of horrible circumstances because their work is unseen and often unfelt. I believe we do harm to our faith when we try to answer questions not answered in God's Word. It is clear that angels don't prevent disaster, disease, and death, else there would be none. I receive their ministry, but I never question God and His wisdom.

There are holy angels, and there are fallen angels. All of them were created as holy angels, but a third of them rebelled against God and fell from their sinless position. It is important to remember that Satan, the leader of these demons, is a liar, a murderer, and a thief (John 8:44; 10:10). He hates God, and he passionately hates God's people. The Bible tells us that he prowls around like a roaring lion, seeking whom he may devour (1 Pet. 5:8). We need to remember that Satan and all the demons are supernaturally brilliant, and Satan can disguise himself as an angel of light (2 Cor. 11:14).

Angels and the New Age Philosophy

There seems to be a flood of misinformation and interest in angels in the New Age philosophy that magnifies man. It's this masquerade as a holy angel that is behind the current angel craze in our culture. While there are a number of wonderful Christian books available that relate stories of holy angels helping people, there are many books, publications, and seminars that are filled with demonic deception of the ugliest kind. When you start talking to angels, you end up dealing with demons. Let me repeat that: when you are talking to angels, you are dealing with demons!

The enemy of our soul is using a new twist on an old lie, exploiting the current interest in angels to attract the unsaved, the untaught, and the undiscerning. Much of the current angel mania is simply New Age philosophy, which is actually old-fashioned pantheism. Pantheism is the belief that everything, an impersonal God as well as every part of the creation, is one big unity. All is one. God is one; we are God. Much of the New Age philosophy includes belief in reincarnation.

You can identify these nonbiblical philosophies when you see or hear these terms:

Contacting or communing with angels

There are now books available with titles like *Ask Your Angels* and *100 Ways to Attract Angels*. However, the Bible gives neither permission nor precedent for contacting angels. When people start calling on angels, it's not the holy angels who answer. They're demons, disguising themselves as good angels to people who don't know how to tell the difference.

Loving our angels or praying to our angels

These false and dangerous teachings instruct their followers to love their angels and call upon them for health, healing, prosperity, and guidance. But angels are God's servants, and all this attention and emphasis and glory should go to God, not His servants. God says, "I am the LORD...and my glory will I not give to another" (Isa. 42:8). Scripture makes no mention of loving angels—only of loving God, His Word, and people. It never tells us to pray to angels, only to the Lord Himself. No holy angel would ever seek to be loved or glorified. Never!

Instruction, knowledge, or insight from angels, particularly ones with names

These ideas and teachings come from those who seek self-glory and are led by demon spirits. Some "angel teachers" are proclaiming that angels are trying very hard to contact us so they can give us deeper knowledge of the spiritual. Invariably this "angel knowledge" is a mixture of truth and lies, and it never stands up to the absolute truth of Scripture. This is the ultimate and only measuring instrument for truth—God's Holy Word.

Special knowledge or teachings from angels

One of the best-known and most foolish lie of fallen angels is that about the so-called angel Moroni, who supposedly brought new, updated information from heaven. It is moronibaloney. There are false teachings about the deep meanings of colors and numbers and letters of the alphabet, which one of the New Age philosophers claims is "knowledge given from above and brought forth in more detail by the High Angelic Master Sheate, Lady Master Cassandra, and Angel Carpelpous, and the Master Angel, One on High."[1] These same beings are reportedly said to stress two main teachings: first, that God accepts all religions, and second, reincarnation. These two teachings keep showing up in much of the New Age angel literature. Special knowledge from angels is entertaining the lies of demons.

Human divinity

This New Age teaching suggests that we need to recognize that we are one with the divine, we are divine—we are God. What pathetic and demonically inspired teaching! Also much of the angel literature refers to "the angel within." But angels are a separate part of the creation. They were created before man as a different kind. They are not within us.

Here are some indelible truths concerning angels:

1. The ministry of holy angels will never contradict the Bible.

2. The actions of holy angels will always be consistent with the character of Christ.

3. A genuine encounter with a holy angel will glorify God, not the angel. Holy angels never draw attention to themselves. They typically do their work and disappear.

It's very true that we have "entertained angels unawares" (Heb. 13:2). But we need to make sure we're entertaining the right kind of angels!

Chapter 15

WHERE DO DEMONS PREFER?

IN THE PARABLES Jesus shared in Matthew 13, some incredible insight into the heavenly realm is touched upon in verse 19: "When any one heareth the word of the kingdom, and understandeth it not, then cometh the wicked one, and catcheth away that which was sown in his heart. This is he which received seed by the way side."

If you hear or see something, it is registered in the mind. In this verse Jesus said that if it is not well received, then comes the "wicked one" and steals it away. Now since Satan is not omnipresent and cannot be in all places at all times, who is it that steals away the Word from the mind of man? It is his demon powers, and it seems clear that they must have access to what is received in our minds.

One of my favorite commentators, Matthew Henry, says:

> The *wicked one,* that is, the devil, *cometh and catcheth away that which was sown.* —Such mindless, careless, trifling hearers are an easy prey to Satan; who, as he is the great murderer of souls, so he is the great thief of sermons, and will be sure to rob us of the word, if we take not care to keep it: as the birds pick up the seed that falls on the ground that is neither ploughed before nor

harrowed after. If we break not up the fallow ground, by preparing our hearts for the word, and humbling them to it, and engaging our own attention; and if we cover not the seed afterwards, by meditation and prayer; if we give not a *more earnest heed to the things which we have heard,* we are as the highway ground. Note, The devil is a sworn enemy to our profiting by the word of God; and none do more befriend his design than heedless hearers, who are thinking of something else, when they should be thinking of the things that belong to their peace.[1]

When evil spirits get into the mind of man, what is actually happening? The psyche of man is so complicated that it is difficult to draw conclusions. I don't suppose anyone can say conclusively what the mind is. The brain is obviously part of our physical makeup, but does it include the mind? Is it the mind? Is the subconscious a separate part of the brain or of the mind? What is the subconscious?

One online encyclopedia gives this definition: "The term subconscious is used in many different contexts and has no single or precise definition. This greatly limits its significance as a definition-bearing concept, and in consequence the word tends to be avoided in academic and scientific settings."[2]

Do demons actually get into the mind? First, what is the difference between the conscious and subconscious? It seems that the subconscious mind is made up of everything one sees or hears as well as life experiences. Maybe it's like a *flash drive* where information is stored so it can be retrieved by the conscious mind when it is needed.

When God breathed life into man and he became a living soul, that breath separated us from all the rest of His creation. I believe the soul is uniquely attached to the spirit of man. It is in the mind where spiritual battles take place. What is the "mind of Christ" in a believer? It is the mind of a person who has experienced the new birth and is energized by the Holy Spirit.

Look at 1 Corinthians 2:14–16 (NKJV):

> But the natural man does not receive the things of the Spirit of God, for they are foolishness to him; nor can he know them, because they are spiritually discerned. But he who is spiritual judges all things, yet he himself is rightly judged by no one. For "who has known the mind of the LORD that he may instruct Him?" But we have the mind of Christ.

The unsaved man is not able to receive the things of the Spirit of God. That is exactly what the Word of God says. I would further say that a man who carries unconfessed sin can hardly receive the things of the Spirit of God. When demons have access to our mind, it becomes clouded with lies. Here is something that evolutionists do not like. How is it that man has a distinct advantage over all creation by having a mind?

Ask yourself, why does man have so many distinctive characteristics? Animals don't laugh; no other creature is able to appreciate, create, and express humor. Humor requires creativity and an appreciation of creativity. Man is absolutely unique. My dog, Ellie, doesn't laugh at my jokes, and she's never told me one. At least if she has, I didn't get it.

What about appreciation of beauty or handiwork? Man is able to appreciate all kinds of beauty. This can be as simple as a sunset, a work of art, or the intricate design of a flower. If I take my dog to Ranger Stadium to see a baseball game, she will be interested in the crowd and the smell of hot dogs, but she will have no ability to appreciate the architecture and magnitude of the ballpark. Neither will she be able to recognize the skill involved to play the game.

And look at the wonder of self-consciousness. We are able to look at our past, present, and future; analyze our situation; and make an intelligent decision. How can one explain mental capacities of man versus animals and not see that we are a living soul because God made us that way? Animals can understand simple words or tones, but they do not comprehend syntax or communicate in complex sentences. Human beings have hundreds of languages with thousands of dialects, even though we are born with limited means with which to communicate.

Humans can wonder, speculate, and search the annals of history for lessons and apply those lessons to goals far into the future Animals are only able to relate time to themselves; they have no ability of relating time to third parties. I've never seen an animal with a watch or a laptop. They only have the ability to know by instinct and repetition of events.

While animals have a survival instinct and sometimes intense desire to live, they are not able to consider that one day they will die. In fact, nearly all cultures perform some form of funeral ritual. This is not found in the animal world. Man is aware that his days will not last forever and has a deep respect of his mortality.

How can we be so far above all of creation if we just evolved? Animals are not able to question the meaning of life. No animal contemplates its reason for living. Man is able to adapt to his surroundings. We wear clothes, build shelters, or modify our environment to suit our needs. Animals don't build hospitals.

Animals always take the path of least resistance. Man can decide to find a better way. Man has a conscience or sense of right and wrong. Mankind will go so far as to control his thoughts based on what he considers right or wrong. Man has the ability to know right from wrong, and turn from the wrong and do what is right, even in the face of pressures and temptations. The desire to build character is only found in man. If this is not enough, unlike animals, man can deviate from his course of thinking and living however he sees fit. Animals react through instinct.

The mind of man has the capacity for wisdom. However, animals without the ability to place themselves in time are unable to weigh situations with previous experiences. While animals are able to develop behavioral patterns based on positive or negative stimulation, they are completely unable to analyze actions before they are performed. This ability, known as wisdom, is unique to human beings.

Perhaps the most distinguishing difference is man's desire to worship. No matter what part of the world or culture, man exhibits a desire to seek, follow, and worship a higher power. Animals do not. While some animals form lifelong relationships for the purpose of reproduction, none exhibit a parallel with the human characteristics of love, in which a couple shares experiences, goals, dreams, hopes, and aspirations.

It is always true that several people can witness the same event and have different conclusions of what took place, especially in the area of detail. Our human senses also can have varied strengths and weaknesses. The five basic senses are touch, taste, sight, hearing, and smell. From these basic senses perception is formed and conclusions are reached in the brain.

I recently had a deliverance session with a man from one of our western states. He loved the Lord and desperately wanted to be free from demon spirits. He was also puzzled by some bizarre happenings in his life. He was very genuine in his quest for freedom. One of the many things he shared with me was seeing demons in dreams, and the demons would come out of his body and stare back at him. They are "horrible looking creatures," he said. "Don, I have seen them also in my house at times."

As we got into the deliverance, there was a particular demon who claimed responsibility for him seeing into the spirit realm. I won't mention the demon's name, but he said, "I am in his senses and affect his perception." I find this very interesting. The very definition of perception is, "the ability to see, hear, or become aware of something through the senses." Wouldn't this be the best place to deceive us—in our minds, our senses? Perception deception! Demons are masters of it.

Dreams, drug-induced hallucinations, and so much more are beyond our ability to comprehend. If you were Satan or one of his demon powers, where would you focus your attack upon a human being? Me too; I'd go for the mind.

Always Looking

A few months ago I went with one of our ministry team members to eat lunch. This was at a hamburger restaurant near our office in Colleyville, Texas. We and other members of our team eat there often. This was an unusual day. While we don't know any of the workers there personally, we always greet each other with a smile. While we were eating, one of the workers, a young girl, walked over to our table. She paused and then said to me, "Do you pray for people?"

I'm sure she had noticed that our group always bowed to give thanks before we ate. What a testimony this is; I assure you people are watching, and they can't help but think about what you are doing. Maybe there was another reason she came to me, I'm not sure, and maybe God was answering the deeper cries of her heart. Maybe an angel directed her to me; surely the Holy Spirit was involved.

I remember being with a friend in Las Vegas once. He is a Christian businessman and invited me to go on a trip with him. He promised to play golf while we were there if I would go. Neither of us really wanted to be in Las Vegas. I recall being in a restaurant with him, and after we had given thanks, we both sort of looked at each other with a grin. "They probably think we are smelling our food," he said. We still laugh about that.

This young girl in Colleyville, I will call Laura, certainly surprised me with the question she asked me: "Do you pray for people?"

"Yes, I do," I said. "Do you have a special prayer need?"

"I'm going to interview for a job tomorrow," she said, "and I really need the job because I don't have hardly any money."

I assured her I would pray for her. I asked, "What kind of job is it? What will you be doing?"

She said, without a blink or a blush, "It's nude modeling."

"Nude modeling!" I said, "Does your mom know about this?"

She told me she had spoken with her mom who lived on the West Coast, and she had no problem with it. (I later found out that her mom was a lesbian and had raised her with another lesbian in the home.) "She doesn't really care," she said.

"But you care, don't you?" I said. "That is not what you really want to do, is it?"

She replied with, "They said they would pay me one hundred dollars if I would do it."

I said, "I'll give you a hundred dollars not to do it."

She hesitated, thought a minute, and said, "No, you wouldn't."

The worker seated with me, who had been silent the whole time, spoke up, "Yes, he will." I happened to have a one hundred dollar bill with me, and I took it from my billfold to give to her.

Because it was busy, I could not really witness to her at that time. She did take the money, and I told her we would come back the next day. The following morning in our office I mentioned this and asked our team members to pray for her.

I said, "We are going back there today, and I'll take a few gospel tracts."

One of the ladies in our office who was training for deliverance ministry spoke up, "I'm all over this! I'm all over this, and I'm going with you." (She had been saved and rescued from the adult entertainment industry herself; she knew how it all worked.)

Betty* was excited at the opportunity to witness to this girl. She talked with her privately for a few minutes and told her, "I'll pick you up at 5:00 p.m." She had invited her to a Bible study that evening. She gave her a Bible and witnessed to her about the love and saving power of Jesus Christ. Laura was saved that night! The next time I went to that restaurant, Laura saw me coming and greeted me at the door with a big hug, "Thank you for praying for me. Thank you," she said. She seemed not only happy but also relieved.

Not long after that, she transferred to a location that was closer to her home. I haven't seen her since. You know, I don't think she even knows my name.

The Book of Mark mentions that one day Jesus sat by the treasury and watched as the people gave (Mark 12:41). I'm guessing He still does. In fact, the phrase "the eyes of the Lord" appears no less than twenty-one times in the Bible. While this

---

* Not her real name

is hard to understand in one way, it is wonderfully clear when we remember that God is omnipotent and omniscient, as well as omnipresent. "He that formed the eye, shall he not see?" (Ps. 94:9). Look at Proverbs 15:3: "The eyes of the LORD are in every place, beholding the evil and the good." Angels look. Demons look. God looks. People look!

While we can know with greater certainty that God looks, angels are looking for ways to minister for us; sometimes this comes simply by speaking words of faith. They are watching over us. Demons are watching for opportunities of evil— sometimes this comes from simply speaking words of hatred, anger, and bitterness. They lurk in shadows and darkness, but they are looking.

Lots of eyes watching; you can be sure that people are looking. Little children are looking. People in the car behind you are looking. People in the restaurant are looking. Jesus was likely watched more than any other man. They watched in order to find fault, but they couldn't. They watched to trick Him and trap Him, but they couldn't. They watched His miracles and wanted to be touched by Him, and they were!

I think it is a fair statement that most people are looking for love and genuineness, even though people are often looking in the wrong places. I'm not sure why people might be watching you and me, but you can be sure they are.

Heavenly Places

> Blessed be the God and Father of our Lord Jesus Christ, who hath blessed us with all spiritual blessings in heavenly places in Christ: according as he hath chosen us in him before the foundation of the world, that we should be holy and without blame before him in love.
>
> —EPHESIANS 1:3–4

The spiritual realm is as real as the natural realm. In fact the spiritual realm, in many ways, determines what takes places in the natural realm. While the location of heaven is up high above the earth, its operation is all over the earth and in our hearts.

> And when he had spoken these things, while they beheld, he was taken up; and a cloud received him out of their sight. And while they looked stedfastly toward heaven as he went up, behold, two men stood by them in white apparel; which also said, Ye men of Galilee, why stand ye gazing up into heaven? this same Jesus, which is taken up from you into heaven, shall so come in like manner as ye have seen him go into heaven.
> —ACTS 1:9–11

When Jesus ascended up into heaven, He was received, perhaps escorted, by His angels into heaven, and a couple of the angels stayed to give a word to the Upper Room assembly. These two angels were clothed in white and came from the heavenly realm. They would also ascend shortly back into that realm, but first they announced the greatest news since the resurrection. He's coming back. This same Jesus is coming back and is coming back the same way you have seen Him leave!

The Bible does not say that Jesus ascended by His own power *like a rocket* but rather that He was *taken* up. He was also received by a cloud, or in a cloud. What is taking place in this mysterious realm, far beyond our abilities to conceive? We see into the realm by faith. Remember the story of Elisha and his fearful servant in 2 Kings 6:16. The troubled servant feared for their death, but Elisha spoke: "Fear not: for they that be with us are more than they that be with them. And

Elisha prayed, and said, LORD, I pray thee, open his eyes, that he may see. And the LORD opened the eyes of the young man; and he saw: and, behold, the mountain was full of horses and chariots of fire round about Elisha" (vv. 16–17).

As a believer, that is always the case. There are more with us than against us. We cannot see into this dimension of the heavenly realm. That's one of the reasons we are admonished to walk by faith and not by sight. Our provision and protection are in the heavenly realm. As a matter of fact, *all spiritual blessings* originate in the heavenly realm.

Our correct thinking and our incorrect thinking are influenced by the heavenly realm. Look at the Book of James:

> Who is a wise man and endued with knowledge among you? let him shew out of a good conversation his works with meekness of wisdom. But if ye have bitter envying and strife in your hearts, glory not, and lie not against the truth. This wisdom descendeth not from above, but is earthly, sensual, devilish. For where envying and strife is, there is confusion and every evil work. But the wisdom that is from above is first pure, then peaceable, gentle, and easy to be intreated, full of mercy and good fruits, without partiality, and without hypocrisy.
>
> —JAMES 3:13–17

There is a wisdom that is earthly, sensual, and demonic. It produces envy, strife, confusion, and every evil work. Demonic wisdom is actually thinking that produces sin and rebellion against God. Remember that is the purpose of Satan and his demons—oppose all that is of God; war against believers. That is deceitful demonic thinking; it is demonic wisdom from the heavenly realm.

Contrast that with genuine godly wisdom. Wisdom in the

context here is a thought process. It is thinking that is generated by yielding to God's Holy Spirit and receiving from Him, or closing one's self to the Holy Spirit and receiving from demons and fleshly desires. There is great activity in the spirit realm, and we participate regardless. We are the focus of spirit realm activity.

Our spiritual thinking is based upon our agreement with God's Word or our rebellion against its truth—maybe ignorance of God's Word fits here also. Satan and his demon powers are mind blinders. The god of this world has a purpose of blinding the mind to truth. Have you ever experienced this—you are ready to go into a serious prayer time and all of a sudden, from out of nowhere comes a most ungodly thought. What is this? I'm pretty sure many of you have experienced this.

Maybe you have decided to devote some time in Bible study, and the phone rings or something similar distracts you. What do you think this is? Would demonic heavenly realm spirits be opposed to you getting closer to God? Is this kind of activity really taking place in the heavenly realm, the dimension we cannot see? Do they really transmit thoughts to our minds? Absolutely!

Do you not think that our thoughts are influenced by spirits? Remember when Jesus asked the disciples who men said that He was, and Peter ultimately said, "Thou art the Christ, the Son of the living God" (Matt. 16:16). Jesus immediately told him that flesh and blood did not reveal that to him, but the Father who is in heaven brought the revelation. Peter received the truth by the Spirit Himself.

But look how quickly Peter was influenced by demonic thinking. Jesus actually said to him, "Get thee behind me, Satan" (v. 23). Jesus was revealing to His disciples that He indeed was the Christ, and giving them some detail. Look at Matthew 16:21–23 (NKJV):

> From that time Jesus began to show to His disciples that He must go to Jerusalem, and suffer many things from the elders and chief priests and scribes, and be killed, and be raised the third day. Then Peter took Him aside and began to rebuke Him, saying, "Far be it from You, Lord; this shall not happen to You!" But He turned and said to Peter, "Get behind Me, Satan! You are an offense to Me, for you are not mindful of the things of God, but the things of men."

How quickly Peter's mind was influenced by a different spirit. It seemed like he was only saying how much he loved Jesus, but he said it out of fleshly, devilish, soulish thinking. He received a severe rebuke! Maybe he spoke too soon, perhaps without trying the spirit to see if it be of God. I'm pretty sure I may have reacted the same way. But Jesus was telling him that he was not able to receive what He just told him: "I must go unto Jerusalem, and suffer many things of the elders and chief priests and scribes, and be killed, and be raised again the third day." If it is the Word of God, it is always best to believe it, regardless. If Jesus says, "I must," we'd best not question it.

Man's Heart

Look how quickly, how easily our minds can be influenced. There are signals going out all of the time; communication is being directed toward our minds, toward our hearts. Is the soul of man different from the *heart* of man? The Bible has much to say about the heart of man.

According to *Strong's Concordance* the word *heart* is mentioned in the King James Version of the Bible 830 times. Knowing about the heart of man is thus a massive study, and I might add from a human point of view, it is a complex one. God knows all of our hearts. "Then hear in heaven Your dwelling place, and forgive, and act, and give to everyone according to all his ways, whose heart You know (for You alone know the hearts of all the sons of men)" (1 Kings 8:39, NKJV).

It seems that when the Bible speaks of the human heart, it is speaking of the thinking of a man, a man's will, a man's emotions or feelings, a man's conscience, or any given combinations of these. We all know that it is not referring to the physical organ that pumps blood and life through our body. Likely the word may have reference to the whole inner being of man combining all the elements that make up the man.

There are many, many verses that indicate that the heart is the thinking aspect of man. Here's a few:

> For as he thinks in his heart, so is he.
> —PROVERBS 23:7, NKJV

> But Jesus, knowing their thoughts, said, "Why do you think evil in your hearts?"
> —MATTHEW 9:4, NKJV

> For out of the heart proceed evil thoughts.
> —MATTHEW 15:19, NKJV

> But if that evil servant says in his heart, "My master is delaying his coming…"
> —MATTHEW 24:48, NKJV

> But Mary kept all these things and pondered them in her heart.
> —LUKE 2:19, NKJV

Mary *thought* about these things and mulled them over in her mind. It seems biblically clear that the heart is the place of thought, reasoning, and understanding within man.

Then would the heart be *the will* of man? Certainly it includes the will of man. We can hardly separate the will from thought. While closely connected, it seems the will of man provides the determination to carry out the thought. I'm not sure there is much spiritual advantage to try to define our makeup. I believe a strong will is good when directed by God. Being of a strong will when directed by truth and love is a godly characteristic.

The heart of man also includes our feelings and emotions. It is the deep part of our being. It is with the heart that we experience joy and sorrow, gladness or regret. The heart is a man's conscience. When Peter preached on the Day of Pentecost, the Bible says that many who heard him "were cut to the heart" (Acts 2:37, NKJV). They felt guilty. Their conscience was bothering them.

The heart and the mind are complexly intertwined, yet we say things like, "My heart says yes, but my mind says no." It seems we are saying, "My emotions and feelings say yes, but my intellect says no." We all understand this. Jesus made a distinction somewhat when He addressed the great commandment question.

> Master, which is the great commandment in the law? Jesus said unto him, Thou shalt love the Lord thy God with all thy heart, and with all thy soul, and with all thy mind. This is the first and great commandment. And the second is like unto it, Thou shalt love thy neighbour as thyself. On these two commandments hang all the law and the prophets.
> —MATTHEW 22:36–40

Heart, soul and mind! There is so much more that can be said. If you were Satan or one of his demon powers, where would you attack? As I stated previously, me too; I'd go for the mind, will, and emotions. I'd go for the heart.

Chapter 16

SLEEPLESS IN SEATTLE

W E HAD A recent Night of Ministry in the Dallas-Fort Worth area. A Night of Ministry is really just that, structured much like a typical church worship service, but the focus is not just talking about healing and deliverance but actually ministering in those areas. Years ago after experiencing many of these types of miracles in the prisons, I would return home to find that it was going to be church as usual. Many of you know what I mean. No one was healed, no one was delivered, no mention of it in the classrooms or the pulpit.

I wondered why these things were happening in the prison services and other places where I preached but not in the churches. I was most often in the pew on Sunday mornings if I was in town. I began to see that not only was it not happening, but also no one wanted it to happen. People would even *shrink away* when I talked about it. It wasn't just my local church; it wasn't happening anywhere that I knew about. I was experiencing God's hand and supernatural power in my prison services, but the message was not readily accepted in local churches... it's still not. People liked to hear the stories, but often it was with a raised eyebrow. I continue to find that people are satisfied with church as usual. That's a criticism, but it's not directed at anyone personally. That's another story, and it's one I addressed in my book *When Pigs Move In*.

This is how a Night of Ministry came about. I said to myself, "Why not just have meetings and let that be the focus?" We began doing this quarterly in our area and whenever invited in other parts of the country. I preach for twenty to thirty minutes about what God's Word teaches in this area, and then have a corporate deliverance and an altar call. We see many people delivered and healed. Generally a corporate deliverance does not produce full freedom. Sometimes it does. Personal individual deliverance brings personal individual freedom.

People travel from long distances to attend these meetings, hoping and expecting to receive from the Lord. At the previously noted meeting in Dallas-Fort Worth, a family had come from the state of Washington. They flew in the day of the service and brought their nine-year-old son to the meeting. I met them prior to the service, but I didn't know them otherwise. On this particular night something special happened. Read the Scripture passage below:

> Then He went down to Capernaum, a city of Galilee, and was teaching them on the Sabbaths. And they were astonished at His teaching, for His word was with authority. Now in the synagogue there was a man who had a spirit of an unclean demon. And he cried out with a loud voice, saying, "Let us alone! What have we to do with You, Jesus of Nazareth? Did You come to destroy us? I know who You are—the Holy One of God!" But Jesus rebuked him, saying, "Be quiet, and come out of him!" And when the demon had thrown him in their midst, it came out of him and did not hurt him. Then they were all amazed and spoke among themselves, saying, "What a word this is! For with authority and

power He commands the unclean spirits, and they come out." And the report about Him went out into every place in the surrounding region.

Now He arose from the synagogue and entered Simon's house. But Simon's wife's mother was sick with a high fever, and they made request of Him concerning her. So He stood over her and rebuked the fever, and it left her. And immediately she arose and served them.

When the sun was setting, all those who had any that were sick with various diseases brought them to Him; and He laid His hands on every one of them and healed them. And demons also came out of many, crying out and saying, "You are the Christ, the Son of God!"

—Luke 4:31–41, nkjv

"When the sun was setting, all those who were sick...with various diseases..."—that is a description of our Night of Ministry. On this particular evening I preached about the woman who had been bound with a spirit of infirmity for eighteen years from Luke 13. However, as I had prepared for this message, the Holy Spirit had put things on my heart that would normally not find their way into my message. I actually mentioned some things that I am writing about now. I mentioned different *dimensions* and a theory I had read about in a *quantum physics* article that if a proton is small enough, it can actually exist in two different places at the same time. I preached about the mind and heart of man and where I would attack if I was a demon. I even wondered as I was preparing my message why I was reading about this.

We went through the service, and there was not anything unusual until we came to the corporate deliverance. I led the congregation through a public prayer, confessing Jesus was Lord. We confessed unforgiveness, anger, bitterness, and so on. We denounced generational sin and renounced unholy oaths, vows, pledges, and ceremonies. We denounced unholy soul ties and confessed them as sin. I then explained that I was going to bind evil spirits and command them to go. As I did that, the nine-year-old boy began to *screech*, almost like the sound of a wild bird scared for its life. He slid from his second row seat out and under the front row. His father picked him up and took him to a small room adjacent to the platform. I continued to minister to the people, and many received deliverance and healing. As members of our ministry team prayed with others, I went to where the little boy was. He was still screaming and somewhat out of control.

Deliverance for Eric

I prayed for him. I commanded demons to leave him, but he resisted. He twisted and turned and didn't want anyone touching him. He kept saying, "No, leave me alone." He was on his hands and knees facing the wall. He resisted for almost an hour; no one held him or restrained him. (This is never acceptable.) You don't take the demonic kingdom by force but by love and through the name of Jesus. It is never a power encounter. I talked to him; I think we became friends, and the screaming stopped. His father knelt beside him and confessed that he may have been the doorway for demons because he had disciplined too hard a few years ago. He wept and asked God to forgive him and laid his hand on his son's back and asked for his forgiveness. His father told me that his son changed after the traumatic time of discipline and had become very uncontrollable.

I continued and asked Eric* to say, "Leave me alone in the name of Jesus."

He shook his head and said, "No, I won't say it."

As we talked, I asked him why he wouldn't say that. He quickly went to my sermon. He's a little genius, and he said, "Can a proton really be two places at the same time?"

I said, "I don't know, Eric. I read that somewhere."

"Do you know about quantum physics?" he asked.

I told him I barely knew what it was and that he might know more about it than me.

He said, "Can you prove to me that this will work?"

I told him that I had never known it not to.

He was becoming much calmer, but he would not say the name Jesus. He refused. I asked him if he was afraid to say it, and he gave a little nod. He could "see" the demon in his mind; he described it as a creature that lived in the very deep part of the sea. He said it was ugly and had little tentacles that came out from its body.

I told him I knew who it was, that it was a leviathan spirit and that it would not hurt him. I said, "I have encountered that kind of spirit many times." I told him that the demon spirit was afraid of the name of Jesus. He gave another little nod. (Leviathan is not a demon's name; it is a type of demon.)

Still he would not say it. He said, "If I was in the fifth dimension, I could do this myself." I agreed with him and told him that Jesus could do it now. Eric said, "I feel like if I say it, my heart will explode and go into a million pieces and out into space." He said his heart was jumping up and down like it was on a trampoline. The demon spirit was instilling as much fear as possible, but it was the demon who was scared. Eric continued to change the subject; he said, "I can't see my

---

* Not his real name

watch in here; it's too dark. Then he said, "Is it true that dark-ness doesn't exist, that it is just the absence of light?" (I had mentioned that in my message.)

We talked about the Dallas Cowboys and the Seattle Seahawks. We talked, and his dad stood near him and wept; his mom was outside of the small hallway-type room. Many people were still in the building being prayed for, and I'm sure many were praying for Eric. I said, "Eric, you are a very smart guy; can you just tell me why you can't say, 'Leave me in the name of Jesus'? Why do you suppose you can't say that?"

He pondered and said, "We'll wait it out."

He began to rub his hands in rapid fashion and said, "I think I can burn it out." Then he said, "No, that's not going to work. We'll just wait it out."

We continued to talk, and I said, "Eric, do you know who Jesus is?" He was silent. I said, "Do you know who God is?"

"Yes, I have a Bible. I know who He is."

I continued to appeal to his reason. "You still haven't told me why you think it is so difficult for you to say that."

His dad said, "Son, you are so close; can you just say those words?"

His little heart was pounding; this spirit had a deep hold on his life and did not want to leave. I said, "Eric, you'll sure make your mom and dad happy, and you will also be happy."

After a minute or so I asked him if he wanted me to hold his hand while he said it. He paused and said, "Maybe if I hold hands with my mom and dad I can say it." His mom came into the room. She had been listening, and she took Eric's right hand, and his dad was holding his left hand. Eric had his head bowed, and I said, "Eric, just say what I say." I repeated, "Leave me alone in the name of Jesus."

He got the first part out easily but began to struggle; his

voice sounded like he was being choked. He got through "name" but could hardly say "Jesus." He got it out and said, "I am feeling like Jello on the inside." He breathed out several deep sighs, and he was no longer trembling. He said, "I think I'm going to throw up."

I told him he could if he needed to.

He said, "I think it's OK. I don't need to."

After the service people lingered, but I was able to get to the door to speak with a few people as they left. Eric came by and gave me a high five. But that was not the end. On Tuesday we received the following e-mail in our office:

> Pastor Don,
>
> This is Ray and Debbie*—the parents of the little boy Eric whom you prayed for on Saturday. Please, please we desperately need your help! Things are much worse, and he has been savagely tormented for the past two nights. He is vulgar, abusive, and completely out of control. He threatens to kill us and wants to see us in hell with *blisters on our faces*. We have been praying and praying. This has been going on for a year, but is terribly worse now. My wife and I have been plagued by nightmares.... Praise Jesus for His divine protection and the angels who intercede for us! We stepped out in faith for this trip, backed by the prayers of many, many people. We trust our Lord in everything, and we are 100 percent certain of His hand in this. But we are deeply struggling to understand.
>
> We are so very touched and humbled that (at the Lord's prompting) you left the flock to go after the *one* on Saturday. But this is not done. We simply cannot go back to Seattle until Eric has been delivered. Our hearts

---

*   Not their real names

can no longer take the pain Eric's five little brothers are forced to endure day after day. And God has a big plan for Eric's life to bring Him glory!

There is absolutely nothing we would not sacrifice to see our son healed. Will you please help us?

Blessings, Ray and Debbie

What happened? It was obvious that there were still demons tormenting Eric. One left, to be sure, but many did not. I agreed to meet with Eric *only* if his mom and dad would go through deliverance first. They were scheduled to return to the Northwest on Wednesday evening. Both were willing and completed their request for deliverance forms. We planned to meet at 10:30 a.m. on Wednesday. This is an absolute must; generational permissions must be eliminated. It was clear that something left Eric on Saturday night, but something also stayed—much of the demonic kingdom remained.

Now, I would learn more. Eric was nonverbal until age five. He was diagnosed with *Asperger syndrome*. This is an autism spectrum disorder (ASD). Some of its characteristics include difficulties in social interaction, alongside restricted and repetitive patterns of behavior and interests. Now I am not a disorder specialist. My friend Dr. Gregory Jantz of Seattle is a specialist. He wrote the foreword to this book and is the founder of The Center for Counseling, A Place of Hope in Edmund, Washington. I don't know much about medical or physiological issues. I know some scriptural principles and truths. I know God is a God of order. I know a child did not bring these issues upon himself. I believe ancestral permissions are virtually always the source. Medical websites suggest the likelihood of a genetic basis, though there is no known cause. Genetic…generational?

As I reviewed both the mother's and father's request forms,

I noticed some common areas of possible generational curses. Involvement in secret societies was one possible legal right. This included oaths, vows, pledges, and ceremony involvement by the parents. This may seem insignificant to you, but I have found it to be most significant. The legal rights granted by the forefathers are being exercised by demon powers in a child. Many possible legal permissions were explored and denounced, including alcohol, perversion, depression, mental disorders, Catholicism, occult, suicide, irrational fears, and a host of others.

One of our female ministers met with the mother; I met with the father. Eric waited in the main office area and worked puzzles from a book. He visited with our office manager, Cherie.

The father's deliverance was amazing. More than twenty-five demons were identified by name and cast into the abyss. It seems that people associated with deliverance ministry still have a hard time grasping the concept of identifying demons by name. Let's say you are in a courtroom and asked to state your name. You reply, "Humanoid." Do you think that would be acceptable?

No! Again you are asked and your reply is, "Homo sapiens." You are asked again demandingly to reveal your name, and you say, "Primate of the family *Hominidae*." Could you get by with that even though you have technically identified yourself? Hardly. Once again you are instructed to give your name, and you say, "The only extant species of the genus *Homo*." Are you following me?

Suppose you are asked again, and you say, "Electrician." No, that's a description of what you do. Now, in a commanding fashion, you are told to give the name that is on your birth certificate, the name by which you are legally recognized, the name given you by your father and mother. "Oh, you mean specifically who I am?" Demons don't mind being identified as demons. This is why it is so important to identify the demons by the name as recognized by Jehovah God.

In the deliverance session with Eric's father, twenty-five different demon powers came forth with their names, then their demonic function and their permission to be in the father's life. The same thing was going on with the mother in another room. No head spinning. No voice raising. No taking by force. It is a genuine encounter with truth, the lie of the demon versus the truth of God's Word. It is not about power.

I will say this to you in love. Don't ever try to cast out demons against a person's will. Screaming the name of Jesus at them does not work. Even though the name of Jesus is above all names, and demons fear and tremble at that name, it is their legal right that must be canceled.

In Eric's dad I will give you a few of the responses from the demons, but I will not mention their names.

- "I am all over; I control with fear."

- "I am a serpent, and my work is suicide."

- "I am in the gut; I destroyed his appendix."

- "I confuse and cause autism."

- "I am an armadillo in his emotions, and I keep him from relationships."

- "I am a bug in his emotional heart; I am an administrator in the kingdom."

- "I terrorize in the night."

- "I am a destroyer of white blood cells and cause Epstein-Barr."

- "I am a worm of addiction in the mind; I poison his mind and body, and I am the *Jägermonster.*"

- "I am in his thyroid with a grip."

Each of these demonic responses came from demon powers on the inside who had given their *creative* names (names from creation) and were responding under oath by describing their work. This is not unusual; this is the norm. They were all commanded to go into the abyss!

I went back into the main office and asked Eric if he was ready. He was. He was calm and was wearing a University of Texas hat I gave him earlier. We went into the deliverance room where his father was still seated on the couch. Eric sat beside him. I told his dad before Eric came in that I had been praying about the session and had made a note of some twenty names that I had encountered on various occasions that had something to do with autism. I showed him the list. He said, "Oh, my gosh; I heard Eric say that name this morning."

I explained to Eric that he didn't have to do anything, but if he heard names or responses when I gave commands, he could tell me. I told him that the demons would respond through his father, but if he heard something, he could speak up as well. The little guy was ready. The first name out of his mouth was the name at the top of my list! He gave me the name; I didn't suggest it. Eric spilled out twenty-eight names with their demonic functions. He was responding more quickly than I could take notes. This day he didn't struggle with saying the name of Jesus; he was telling them to go in Jesus's name as they were identified.

Another of the evil spirits said his job was "to trick him and to make him jump and kick." One revealed himself as a sea turtle to drag him deeper. About another Eric said, "He's gray and rusty looking, and he eats stuff."

During Eric's session I could sense strong territorial activity. I commanded that all attempts to interfere and hinder his freedom immediately stop and for the highest ranking of these spirits to identify himself by name. Quickly Eric gave me the demon's name. I pursued, and the demon identified his territory as being Mexico. As I was giving command for this demon to leave and return to the heavenly realm, he said, "It won't matter, because [demon's name] is here." After dismissing this demon back into the heavenlies, I commanded the other territorial spirit to identify itself. Eric gave me his name, and the demon power said, "I back up everything; whatever you erase I will put back. Everything is backed up."

What? Wow! I said to this demon, "That may well be your job and your assignment, but in the name of Jesus you will never touch this child again. Now, confess that to be true in Jesus's name."

The demon confessed it as truth, and I commanded it to leave and never return. Soon we were finished; the mom had gained her freedom as well and was waiting in our office area.

I don't think I will soon forget Eric, his big smile, and him leaving that day in his new University of Texas hat and sunglasses. I spoke to his dad the other day. "I did not know it was possible to be this free. Eric is doing very well. We are all enjoying our freedom!" he said.

Chapter 17

JACOB'S LADDER

IN GENESIS 28 we find the story of Jacob's dream of the ladder ascending to heaven. The first thing we can be sure of is that the angels appeared in a dream. "And he dreamed, and behold a ladder set up on the earth, and the top of it reached to heaven: and behold the angels of God ascending and descending on it" (Gen. 28:12). The angels were doing in the dream just as they do now. They come from God's presence to man, and they return. A steady stream of activity goes on in the spirit realm. They move in a dimension we are rarely privileged to see, whether in a vision or a dream.

Read this entire Scripture passage:

> And Jacob went out from Beer-sheba, and went toward Haran. And he lighted upon a certain place, and tarried there all night, because the sun was set; and he took of the stones of that place, and put them for his pillows, and lay down in that place to sleep. And he dreamed, and behold a ladder set up on the earth, and the top of it reached to heaven: and behold the angels of God ascending and descending on it. And, behold, the LORD stood above it, and said, I am the LORD God of Abraham thy father, and the God of Isaac: the land whereon thou liest, to thee will I give it, and to thy seed; and thy seed

shall be as the dust of the earth, and thou shalt spread
abroad to the west, and to the east, and to the north, and
to the south: and in thee and in thy seed shall all the
families of the earth be blessed.

—GENESIS 28:10–14

The Lord still stands above the activity, and it takes place
as a result of His direction. When God is fulfilling a promise,
you can be sure the angels are His agents. After his dream
Jacob said, "Surely the LORD is in this place; and I knew it
not" (v. 16). God was already working. Jacob didn't know it;
most often we don't either. It is when God allows us a spiritual
glimpse that we are awestruck. It is when we look back and
see that we come to a holy realization of God's great provision.

God used this dream to reinforce to Jacob His covenant,
which He had made to Abraham, that the land of Palestine
would be an everlasting inheritance for the people of Israel.
But does Jacob's ladder hold any meaning for the Gentile?
Check this out; this is one Old Testament incident that Jesus
Himself interpreted. In John 1:45 Philip ran to tell his friend
Nathanael that he had found the promised Messiah. Nathanael
was skeptical, but he agreed to come and meet Jesus. The first
words that Jesus spoke to Nathanael were, "Behold an Israelite
indeed, in whom is no guile!" (v. 47). This was quite the opposite of Jacob; there were deceit and trickery in the heart of
Jacob, but not in Nathanael. Look what Jesus said to Nathanael,
making reference to Jacob's dream. "Verily, verily, I say unto
you, Hereafter ye shall see heaven open, and the angels of God
ascending and descending upon the Son of man" (v. 51).

The ladder, then, that Jacob saw in his dream was not a place
but a person. It is the Lord Jesus Christ who stretches from
earth to heaven, connecting man to God. Jesus is the gateway
to heaven, and there is no other (John 14:6). The angels, the

messengers of God, are seen both descending from heaven and ascending from earth. They carry from God His blessings and provisions to those who love Him, and they come back to our Father bearing the prayers and requests of God's children. Yet the highway upon which they travel is none other than Jesus Christ. There is no other road that leads to God.

Jacob didn't know it. No one else is uniquely qualified to stand in the position that Jesus does. The ladder in this dream reaches all the way down to earth, for He is all man. And it rises all the way to heaven, to the very throne of the Father, for He is all God. The Lord Jesus alone stands with one foot in heaven and one foot on earth, bridging the gap between them. He is the ladder by which God reaches down to man and man reaches up to God. Angels minister for us by way of the Lord Jesus.

There is still activity in the realm between heaven and earth; if we could see with our eyes, we would likely be much stronger in our words than Jacob. He was spiritually stunned. Surely, the Lord is in this place! Maybe we could not find words. "Wow!" Isn't that the word we use when we are unable to express our deep astonishment?

Is it possible that Jacob wrestled physically with an angel of God? I mean, did they literally wrestle? Arm-to-arm combat? What is really happening in this all-night match? Remember, Paul told the Ephesians we don't wrestle with flesh and blood, but we wrestle with principalities and powers. In order to get a better picture of what took place, it helps to know, among other things, that Jacob had created for himself some problems. He was a determined man, but in many ways he was ruthless. He was a con artist, a liar, and a manipulator. In fact, the name *Jacob* not only means "deceiver," but also some say it actually means "grabber."

Jacob's story is one of never-ending struggles. In many ways he is like many ex-inmates I know who are constantly making bad decisions, unable or unwilling to consider the consequences. God had promised Jacob that through him would come not only a great nation but also a whole company of nations. He was a man full of fears and anxieties. Here he is at a crossroads in his life. Esau, his brother, has vowed to kill him. All of Jacob's struggles and fears are about to be realized. His cheating, deceiving life was catching up to him. He felt he was treated wrongly by his father-in-law, and he was running from him, only to encounter his embittered brother. Anxious for his very life, Jacob concocted a bribe and sent a caravan of gifts along with his women and children across the River Jabbok in hopes of pacifying his brother. (Today the Jabbok is known as the Zarqa River.)

His conniving ways were no longer working, and Jacob was at the end of his rope. He is physically exhausted, alone in the desert wilderness, and facing sure death. He's powerless to control his fate. It seems he virtually collapses into a deep sleep on the banks of the river. With his father-in-law behind him and Esau before him, he had nowhere to turn, no place to run, and he was too emotionally and physically spent to struggle any longer. Maybe he laid his head upon a rock as he had done in Bethel. Jacob was tired of running, but he did not know what else to do.

I don't know if you have ever been there. I've sure met a lot of people in my many years of prison ministry who never really looked to God until there was no other place to look. Jacob had the promise of God's blessing on his life, but he was a stubborn, selfish man. Running from his family history was one thing; wrestling with God Himself was a different matter altogether.

He wrestled in his spirit. That night an angelic stranger visited Jacob. They wrestled throughout the night until daybreak, at which point the angel crippled Jacob with a supernatural blow to his hip that disabled him with a limp for the rest of his life. It seems that it was only then that Jacob knew what had happened. He said, "I have seen God face to face, and my life is preserved" (Gen. 32:30). Though we know that a measure of vulnerability, fear, discouragement, and depression comes with normal lives, we tend to view these as signs of failure or even a lack of faith. It was in Jacob's most fearful moment that he made contact with God.

Sooner or later the cold, hard realism of life catches up with most of us. The story of Jacob pulls us back to reality. Here, in Jacob's encounter, it is the defeat of the human soul at the hands of God. It seems clear that angels from God minister to us in times of deep despair. We see that our hope and help lie not in our own strength but in a genuine encounter with God. We can only imagine what this experience was for Jacob, but we do know that no human being could physically defeat an angel. We wrestle in our minds and heart all the time. Jacob knew he could not turn loose of this encounter with God. When you have been in close contact with the Spirit of God, you do not want to have anything else, nor do you want to turn loose. Jacob wanted more of what he knew he needed.

Jacob succeeds in the struggle as he confronts his failures, his weaknesses, his sins, and all the things that are hurting him. He faces God; Jacob wrestled with God all night. It was an exhausting struggle that left him crippled. When Jacob knew and confessed that he could not go on without God's blessing, that is when he realized victory. It seems that in order to convince Jacob of his supernatural power, the angel touched his thigh, which was immediately forced out of joint.

Even then, in bodily pain, Jacob would not give up his earnest efforts. His objective was to obtain a blessing, and pain of body was not sufficient to divert his mind from his desperate need. Jacob's walk was never the same. He triumphed when he surrendered.

But let's peep around the corner and see some more likely details of this wrestling match with an angel. There has always been much spiritual speculation about Jacob's wrestling. Some early rabbinic and modern commentators suggest that the "man" represents Esau in some way, whether Esau himself or Esau's guardian angel. Could this have been an angel assigned to Esau? Could this be an angel sent to bring reconciliation? Could this have been Esau's guardian angel?

The wrestling with Esau began prior to birth. Jacob had wrestled with his twin brother in the darkness of Rebekah's womb:

> And Isaac intreated the LORD for his wife, because she was barren: and the LORD was intreated of him, and Rebekah his wife conceived. And the children struggled together within her; and she said, If it be so, why am I thus? And she went to enquire of the LORD. And the LORD said unto her, Two nations are in thy womb, and two manner of people shall be separated from thy bowels; and the one people shall be stronger than the other people; and the elder shall serve the younger.
>
> —GENESIS 25:21–23

There were not only two nations, which would be Israel and Edom, but two manner of people, two different kinds of people. Certainly that was revealed through their lives and their descendants. Esau and Jacob were born about 1825 BC. The Edomites ceased to be a kingdom about AD 70.

At the river, in Jacob's utter distress, he is nervously anticipating his meeting with his brother the next day. Could it be that the man, the angel, in some sense represents Esau, whether physically, spiritually, or symbolically? Still some Jewish interpretations have seen this as a wrestling match between Israel and the *celestial patron*, or guardian angel of Esau. Recall during the wrestling that Jacob said, "I saw God face to face, and my life is preserved." Notice what he said when he met Esau the next day: "I have seen thy face, as though I had seen the face of God" (Gen. 33:10).

Jacob showed honor and respect toward Esau. Remarkably Esau's countenance and attitude also reflected great change. Something miraculous had happened to both of them. "And Jacob said, Nay, I pray thee, if now I have found grace in thy sight, then receive my present at my hand: for therefore I have seen thy face, as though I had seen the face of God, and thou wast pleased with me" (Gen. 33:10). Maybe he had wrestled with Esau's guardian angel. In some Jewish circles they still hold the belief that a person's guardian angel looks like the person. Perhaps the angel returned to Esau at the break of day, and his heart was changed as well. The angels that come from God's presence always bring something of God's presence with them.

Chapter 18

JESUS SENDS HIS ANGEL

ONE-FOURTH OF ALL the biblical references to angels are in the Book of Revelation. Of its twenty-two chapters, all but three contain references to angels. The Book of Revelation mentions angels sixty-six times, beginning with the very first verse: "The Revelation of Jesus Christ, which God gave unto him, to shew unto his servants things which must shortly come to pass; and he sent and signified it by his angel unto his servant John" (Rev. 1:1). It begins with God the Father giving to Jesus revelation about *end times.* Jesus gave the information to His angel, who gave it to John, who gives it to us. This book, like no other, gives us insight to these majestic creatures and to their duties in obedience to carrying out God's will and purpose. I find it intriguing that Jesus refers to a specific angel as "His" angel. Of course they are all His, but this seems to carry with it a more personal meaning. This is reinforced when He speaks again in the last chapter: "I Jesus have sent mine angel to testify unto you these things in the churches. I am the root and the offspring of David, and the bright and morning star" (Rev. 22:16).

When John saw this, he wanted to worship this angel.

And I John saw these things, and heard them. And when
I had heard and seen, I fell down to worship before the
feet of the angel which shewed me these things. Then
saith he unto me, See thou do it not: for I am thy fel-
lowservant, and of thy brethren the prophets, and of
them which keep the sayings of this book: worship God.
—REVELATION 22:8–9

Angels do not want our worship. Demons do, but not holy
angels. This angel said, "I am your fellow servant. Worship
God." That is a distinctive characteristic of angels; they direct
us to worship God!

Angels refer to themselves as our "fellow servants." I think
that is pretty awesome! We serve the same God in different
ways. We are on the same team.

In the Old Testament we see angels:

- Escorting Lot out of Sodom (Gen. 19:15)

- Slaughtering the enemies of God (2 Kings 19:35)

- Shutting the mouths of lions (Dan. 6:22)

In the New Testament we see them:

- Gathering together God's elect from the four
  winds (Matt. 24:31)

- Rolling away the stone from Jesus's tomb (Matt.
  28:2)

- Delivering a sleeping apostle from prison (Acts
  12:7–10)

- Striking King Herod dead (Acts 12:23)

Let's just look at Acts 12:23. I think this is one of the most intriguing events in Scripture. King Herod was struck, smitten by an angel, and eaten by worms. Wow, what happened here? "And immediately the angel of the Lord smote him, because he gave not God the glory: and he was eaten of worms, and gave up the ghost." I wonder if this was the same angel that released Peter from prison, recorded in the same chapter. One commentator offers this view:

> It was no more than a worm that was the instrument of Herod's destruction: He was eaten of worms...he became worm-eaten, so it must be read; rotten he was, and he became like a piece of rotten wood. The body in the grave is destroyed by worms, but Herod's body putrefied while he was yet alive, and bred the worms which began to feed upon it.[1]

I found a dead body once—a man who had been robbed, shot to death, and dumped in a remote area of a subdivision. The body was being eaten by maggots; the stench was so bad I smelled it from my car as I turned a corner. There is no smell like this. This is the normal thing for a dead body—to be eaten by worms—but Herod was alive when the angel smote him. I don't know if he had a disease. He probably did. But this act by the angel came as a result of Herod receiving praise that belongs only to God!

The acclaimed historian Josephus wrote that in an instant Herod was:

> ...seized with a most violent pain in his bowels, and gripes in his belly, which were exquisite from the very first; that he turned his eyes upon his friends, and said to this purpose: 'Now I, whom you called a god, and

therefore immortal, must be proved a man, and mortal.'
That his torture continued without intermission, or the
least abatement, and then he died in the fifty-fourth year
of his age, when he had been king seven years.[2]

The worms from the disease that he may have had were
now eating his flesh. Pharaoh is plagued with lice and flies.
Ephraim was consumed as with a moth (Hosea 5:12), and
Herod was eaten with worms. The angels are jealous for God,
and this appears to be an act of their jealousy for God and
shows their permission from God to execute judgment.

One thing is clear; we are not able to conceive the might,
power, and vastness of God and His holy creation. We see an
angel with one foot on the sea and one on the land.

> I saw another mighty angel come down from heaven,
> clothed with a cloud: and a rainbow was upon his head,
> and his face was as it were the sun, and his feet as pil-
> lars of fire: and he had in his hand a little book open:
> and he set his right foot upon the sea, and his left foot
> on the earth.
> —REVELATION 10:1–2

This doesn't indicate an angel standing on a beach with one
foot on the sea and one foot on the sand. Rather, it shows a
mighty angel, huge and magnificent, over the land and the
seas. Try to grasp this description: "clothed with a cloud: and
a rainbow was on his head." Look up into the heavens and
picture this. Wow! The angel John saw must have covered the
heavens; his face was like the sun in its brightness and his feet
like pillars of fire.

I think the rapture of the church will be something like this.
I don't believe it will be a "man-sized" Jesus who appears, but
it will be the Lord Himself! Scripture indicates that He will

return as He was seen leaving. Angels told those gathered at His ascension:

> Why do you stand gazing up into heaven? This same Jesus, who was taken up from you into heaven, will so come in like manner as you saw Him go into heaven.
>
> —ACTS 1:11, NKJV

First Thessalonians 4:16–17 (NKJV) tells us:

> For the Lord Himself will descend from heaven with a shout, with the voice of an archangel, and with the trumpet of God. And the dead in Christ will rise first. Then we who are alive and remain shall be caught up together with them in the clouds to meet the Lord in the air. And thus we shall always be with the Lord.

Will He cover the sky? Will His image be seen by all believers? The angel that John saw standing with one foot on the sea and one foot on the land makes me think that the Rapture will be similar. It will be the Lord Himself, not one of His angels. The angels will be active at the Rapture. They are active now.

The Lord Jesus will come down from heaven in all the pomp and power of the upper world. He who ascended into heaven after His resurrection and passed through these material heavens into the third heaven will, when the Father determines, come again and appear in His glory. He will descend from heaven into this our atmosphere. The appearance will be with pomp and power, with the shout of a king, with the power and authority of a mighty king and conqueror, and with the voice of the archangel. Who is this archangel? It has to be Gabriel, right? The Bible doesn't say.

I remember a time when God gave me an instantaneous

glimpse of His coming. I was working and going to school. Our two sons were probably ten and thirteen years old. I had pulled my car over to the side of the road to just pray for a few minutes and to read from a little New Testament I carried with me. I was heavy with some kind of burden, though I don't remember what it was. What I do remember is that during that brief time of prayer, I saw the eastern sky unfold, and an awesome, indescribable scene was revealed. It was so very brief, like a twinkle of the eye.

With that fleeting moment came a peace and excitement that completely erased my trivial heaviness. I don't think I can do that moment justice with any words I can write. It was just a glimpse, ever so brief, but all earthly concerns were erased.

I recall that I was in a very bad part of town, crime ridden with lots of poverty. I don't remember why I was in that location. Looking back, it's certainly not where I would choose to take a break and read my Bible. It had nothing to do with my physical location, of course. The thing I recall most is how insignificant the cares of this world became. It was an exhilarating experience, and I knew it was similar to what it will be when Jesus does appear.

I put my little Bible on the seat next to me and pondered what just happened. I looked again at the eastern sky; I guess I wanted to somehow re-create that moment. It was midmorning and seemed like any other day, but for a fleeting moment I saw something wonderful.

It's kind of like I know now what the Rapture will be like. It will be an event that will cover the sky, not a *human-sized* Jesus or angels the size of men. The whole sky will reveal His glory. The brightness of His image will cover the skies, and, as the Bible says, in a moment, in the twinkling of an eye, we shall be changed. Wow!

When you read through the Revelation of Jesus Christ, you see angels in a much different way. They are powerful, powerful instruments of God to carry out His judgments. They await their time of performing their duties for God. It all has to do with this world, the world that God so loves He sent His only begotten Son. The angels of God are at the door and waiting.

We see that one angel will bind Satan.

> Then I saw an angel coming down from heaven, having the key to the bottomless pit and a great chain in his hand. He laid hold of the dragon, that serpent of old, who is the Devil and Satan, and bound him for a thousand years; and he cast him into the bottomless pit, and shut him up, and set a seal on him, so that he should deceive the nations no more till the thousand years were finished. But after these things he must be released for a little while.
> —REVELATION 20:1–3, NKJV

We see from Scripture that Satan will be cast into the lowest depths of the pit. I guess if you measure from the top downward, Satan will be at the lowest depth. The pit with no bottom is hard to conceive; the deeper and lower part of it is where Satan will be confined for a thousand years. This one mighty angel stands somewhere in eternity awaiting his call, chain in hand.

I wonder what kind of chain he has in his hand. It's obviously not a chain as we know it. Perhaps it's some kind of spiritual chain with which he could restrain another spirit. I like the way Scripture says that this angel "laid hold of" the dragon—this almost seems to be a wrestling term, a headlock or something, maybe more similar to a calf rope and a hog tie. I can't wait to see this!

I believe we will see this. Look at Isaiah's prophecy:

> How art thou fallen from heaven, O Lucifer, son of the morning! how art thou cut down to the ground, which didst weaken the nations! For thou hast said in thine heart, I will ascend into heaven, I will exalt my throne above the stars of God: I will sit also upon the mount of the congregation, in the sides of the north: I will ascend above the heights of the clouds; I will be like the most High. Yet thou shalt be brought down to hell, to the sides of the pit. They that see thee shall narrowly look upon thee, and consider thee, saying, Is this the man that made the earth to tremble, that did shake kingdoms; that made the world as a wilderness, and destroyed the cities thereof; that opened not the house of his prisoners?
> —ISAIAH 14:12–17

Isaiah says about Satan: "Those who see you will gaze at you." Gaze? "They will look at you with fixed eyes, stare intently and studiously at you, consider and say, 'Is this the man? This is the man that shook kingdoms?'" One, just one, of God's holy angels is waiting. The angels are active in the Book of Revelation. They too are looking for His coming. There must be great anticipation in the heavenly realm.

Notes

Introduction
Why Am I Interested?

1. This section relating the encounters the author had in two prison chapel services is adapted from Don Dickerman, *When Pigs Move In* (Lake Mary, FL: Charisma House, 2009), 3–5.

2. Frank Hammond, *Pigs in the Parlor* (Kirkwood, MO: Impact Christian Books, 1973).

Chapter 1
What Are Principalities and Powers?

1. *Vine's Expository Dictionary of New Testament Words*, s.v. "ruler," as viewed at StudyBible.info, "Ruler," http://studybible.info/vines/Ruler (accessed December 13, 2013).

Chapter 2
Insight Into the Demonic Realm

1. Howard O. Pittman, *Demons: An Eyewitness Account* (Philadelphia: Philadelphia Publishing Company, 1995). Used by permission.

2. Ibid.

3. Ibid.

4. Ibid.

5. S. Sanz Fernández de Córdoba, "100km Altitude Boundary for Astronautics," Astronautic Records, *Fédération Aéronautique Internationale*, http://www.fai.org/icare-records/100km-altitude-boundary -for-astronautics (accessed December 16, 2013).

6. The author obtained this account through a personal conversation.

7. Ibid.

8. Marianne Hogan, "The Earth's Inside," http://www.colorado .edu/physics/phys2900/homepages/Marianne.Hogan/inside.html (accessed December 16, 2013).

Chapter 3
The Demons' Favorite Scripture

1. Matthew Henry, *Complete Commentary on the Whole Bible*, s.v. "Matthew Chapter 12," Sacred-Texts.com, http://www.sacred-texts .com/bib/cmt/henry/mat012.htm (accessed December 16, 2013).
2. Ibid.
3. Ibid.

Chapter 5
Are Angels Principalities and Powers?

1. The author received the information in this story from a personal conversation with Eddie Wiese.
2. Matthew Henry, *Commentary on the Whole Bible*, vol. 5, "Mark Chap. 2," Christian Classics Ethereal Library, http://www.ccel.org/ ccel/henry/mhc5.Mark.iii.html (accessed December 16, 2013).

Chapter 6
"Dad, Have You Ever Seen an Angel?"

1. "Shall We Gather at the River?" by Robert Lowry. Public domain.

Chapter 10
Recognizing Their Work in Our Lives

1. Flavius Josephus, *Antiquities of the Jews*, 10.1, viewed at Christian Classics Ethereal Library, http://www.ccel.org/ccel/josephus/ complete.ii.xi.i.html (accessed December 17, 2013).

Chapter 11
Angels From the Throne

1. Billy Graham, *Angels: God's Secret Agents* (Nashville: W Publishing Group, 1995), 30.

Chapter 12
Angelic Activity Surrounding the Birth of Jesus

1. Graham, *Angels: God's Secret Agents*, 37.
2. Other books on the subject by Don Dickerman are *When Pigs Move In* (Lake Mary, FL: Charisma House, 2009) and *Keep the Pigs Out* (Lake Mary, FL: Charisma House, 2010).

Chapter 13
Do Angels Bring Healing?

1. Biblical Archaeology Society Staff, "The Bethesda Pool, Site of One of Jesus' Miracles," Bible History Daily, November 18, 2013, http://tinyurl.com/lglhke7 (accessed December 17, 2013).

2. Ananya Mandal, "Syphilis History," News-Medical.net, http://www.news-medical.net/health/Syphilis-History.aspx (accessed December 17, 2013).

3. John Calvin, *Institutes of the Christian Religion*, book 1, chapter 14, Christian Classics Ethereal Library, http://www.ccel.org/ccel/calvin/institutes.iii.xv.html (accessed December 17, 2013).

Chapter 14
What Angels Are Not

1. This information about a New Age teaching is purposely left unsourced. There is no reason to draw further attention to this untruth.

Chapter 15
Where Do Demons Prefer?

1. Matthew Henry, *Matthew Henry's Commentary on the Whole Bible,* s.v. "Matthew 13," BibleStudyTools.com, http://www.biblestudytools.com/commentaries/matthew-henry-complete/matthew/13.html (accessed December 20, 2013).

2. Encyclo Online Encyclopedia, s.v. "subconscious," http://www.encyclo.co.uk/define/subconscious (accessed December 20, 2013).

Chapter 18
Jesus Sends His Angel

1. Matthew Henry, *Complete Commentary on the Whole Bible*, s.v. "Acts Chapter 12," http://www.sacred-texts.com/bib/cmt/henry/act012.htm (accessed December 20, 2013).

2. Ibid., quoting Josephus, *Antiquities* 19.343–350.

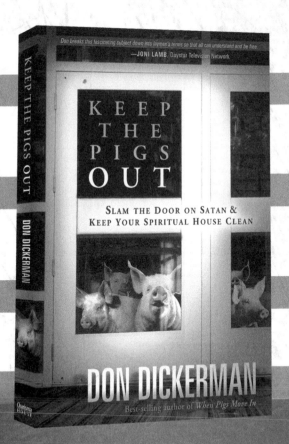

FREE NEWSLETTERS
TO HELP EMPOWER YOUR LIFE

Why subscribe today?

❑ **DELIVERED DIRECTLY TO YOU.** All you have to do is open your inbox and read.

❑ **EXCLUSIVE CONTENT.** We cover the news overlooked by the mainstream press.

❑ **STAY CURRENT.** Find the latest court rulings, revivals, and cultural trends.

❑ **UPDATE OTHERS.** Easy to forward to friends and family with the click of your mouse.

CHOOSE THE E-NEWSLETTER THAT INTERESTS YOU MOST:

- Christian news
- Daily devotionals
- Spiritual empowerment
- And much, much more

SIGN UP AT: **http://freenewsletters.charismamag.com**